1-800-I AM-UNHAPPY

Volume 1

inspirational writs by

CHRIS BENT

Published in the USA by
Chris Bent
Naples, Florida
USA

http://ChrisBent.com

ISBN 978-0-9913328-0-9

1-800-I-AM-UNHAPPY™ is a trademark
owned by Chris Bent
and is used with his permission.

———◆◆◆◆◆———

DEDICATION

To Christina, Candice, Courtney, and their journeys . . .

Prologue

This is meant to be a book for just one person. If just that one person is touched in some way to make their journey better, then the effort is not in vain. Each one of us can look back to one moment that changed our direction for the better. May this book, a collection of my writs and wit, find that pair of eyes.

Chris Bent

Kennebunkport
September 2013
www.ChrisBent.com

Contents

This book is meant to be different and a little strange.
It was never planned. I had written what I call a few "writs"
over the last 10 years. Short pieces that just came in a moment.
I often would get up in the middle of the night and write…
Most all are done in 30 minutes. Go figure?
Where does it come from? I don't know it just flows.
I never knew where the next sentence would go.
I think they are very funny while being as deep as you wish to
go…Each chapter is short, mostly only 500 words
so you can pick up at any time.
These are reflections on our times today and all the challenges
facing us, especially our children…It is your journey…hope I help.
1-800-1 AM-UNHAPPY

inspirational writs by

CHRIS BENT

"The Grenade"

Mike Monsoor was Navy SEAL. Mike won the Congressional Medal of Honor. Mike is dead. You see… He, fellow Seals, and Iraqi soldiers they were working with were on a rooftop on September 29, 2006 in Ramadi. A live grenade appeared. All would be killed or injured. Mike reached deep inside where Truth lives and dove on the grenade. His defining choice. God bless you Mike. Teammates were saved. They hammered their Tridents onto his coffin.

Most of us are never asked to make that kind of decision. Really? I am not so sure. Mike defined choice. He defined what serving is. He chose to serve his buddies with his life. He said there is black and there is white. He said there is evil and there is good. You want to debate??? Then go in the corner and hang an idiot sign around your neck. I'll bring you some animal crackers in an hour.

OK, I feel better. But this is all too important to dismiss quickly. Mike became THE role model of role models in

> *"I did this because of you.*
> *Your example made me do it."*

that instant. The same can be said of Michael Murphy and unseen others...

Every moment of every day something bad happens. Every bad thing is witnessed by someone. Every bad event is initiated by some bad choice. A person is responsible for that choice. Think about it. People make evil possible. A grenade is a really big bad thing. But... what about the small grenades of life? Does a lie ever have the potential to cause great harm? Does a lie actually damage the liar, much less the person who is lied about?

As we all know there are a bunch of sins I could list and there are the famous Commandments I could refer to in helping to define things that cause harm.

And... How about a simple swear word that begins with an "F" uttered in earshot of a young child. The first time that word would ever be heard. Is there any way to know what seed may be planted...of an innocence lost? Would you want that responsibility? Was this not a potential grenade to this young life? Maybe??? Who is to know? In fact every wrong thing we witness in the course of a day is a potential grenade to someone. Maybe we should look at life through Mike's eyes and react with Holy instinct and attack? Or do we out of habit and political correctness look away and busy ourselves with something else… Some work task that is more important? Or maybe turn up the volume of our headphones and sing "Chasing Pavements" along with Adele…??? I want us to give Mike the Medal of Value. That medal can only be created and given to him by our actions. "Here Mike. I did this because of you. Your example made me do it."

I want to be true to my inner core and see more mini-grenades in the course of each day and right them. Stop them in their tracks. To tell the person who perpetrates that they are doing wrong. I want to do it out loud so others hear. Too bad if feelings are hurt. Too bad. Take the criticism and be proud. It matters. Be humble. Every sin is a grenade. Do something about it. Thank you Mike.

"You Know"

You know? I know that you know. Do you know that I know? You know?

Do you know how many times I hear "you know" during the course of the day, week, or YEAR??? I am hoping Bose makes "You Know Ear Plugs" soon. Or headphones that can filter out the "you know" noise. Step up to the plate Dr. Dre.

I was just talking to this teacher and he kept saying "you know." Now I don't know if that was a question or a statement. And if he uses it in class, unconsciously I am sure, then his students will pick it up and proliferate the sales of headphones. You know how many more people are just walking around with headphones, much less ear buds? This is weird. Is society tuning out or tuning in??? How can you hear the fire engine with your headphones on? You certainly can't hear your mother saying "Be careful…"

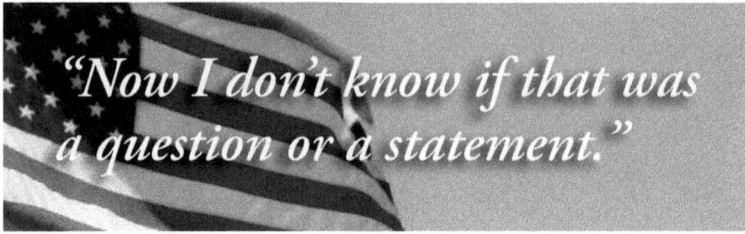

I know that sitting on a sofa with your arm around your girlfriend enjoying your headphones tuned in to the same Adele song is close to heaven. You know? Or for the two geezers in Florida looking at the sunset on the gulf with their silver headphones on reminiscing on the days when the only headphones were in a few recording studios. My friend Bill remembers.

Those were the days when "you know" did not exist. When public schools taught grammar it was called English. Everybody spoke English. Everybody learned about nouns, verbs, adjectives, and adverbs and the correct or traditional way they interplayed with grammar, thought, and expression. Every once in a while you can still hear it if you concentrate with your headphones off. You know?

Then I thought why has the "You Know" (lets acronym it going forward to save typing... phonetic... YN... OK?) cancer spread throughout our proud land? YN seems to imply that you understand what the person is talking about. That you are in synch and agreement. However when you hear the YN you think that you are supposed to understand when you really don't. This puts one at a disadvantage as the perpetrator of the YN has feelings that you wish not to hurt by saying you really don't understand. So you just let it pass and say nothing. Communication has not been established by the use of the YN. In fact communication and trust are slightly diminished.

Now this also allows us to reflect on other ingenious forms of disrespect. How about "How are you doing?", "How's it going?", "What's up?", and "No problem". These infernal insults to politeness are an epidemic as we try to avoid real contact or communication with the pretense of caring and being "cool" with things. They really indicate insecurity. Like verbal sunglasses. YN?

I am for Occupy Bad Grammar Classes (OBGC). Let's protest the way our elite educational system condones and perpetrates bad grammar under the guise of diversity sensitivity or "whatever". Don't get me started on "whatever".

Let's not shave and let's not wear clean clothes. Get your tents and cook stoves and water bottles and head out in groups of six and occupy these bad classrooms a week from Wednesday at 8AM. I know that is early for most, but that is when classes start. YN?

"Supreme Tort"

We finally have the final word from the Supreme Court. Thank God we have somewhere to go to find out what is right and wrong so we can get back to our daily lives. Awaiting their decisions is so exciting as simplicity can be re-established as a cure for the complexities of having a family and growing a business and just having fun.

When things are so much clearer or clarified there will be a better understanding of the rules of life and getting along. Sometimes a current law needs to be tweaked to make both sides happy.

We call the citizens we send to Washington our lawmakers. They debate and decide on how to make our lives so much better and we are always anxious to celebrate their success. But it is all a filibuster on our freedoms as our lives have been put on hold by layers of lawyers litigating liberally.

I am so glad we have a Supreme Tort... Oops... I mean Supreme Court... Sorry... They are the professional arbiters of laws and their simplification. We can relax.

"Where is the 'I Can't Take It Anymore' Movement?"

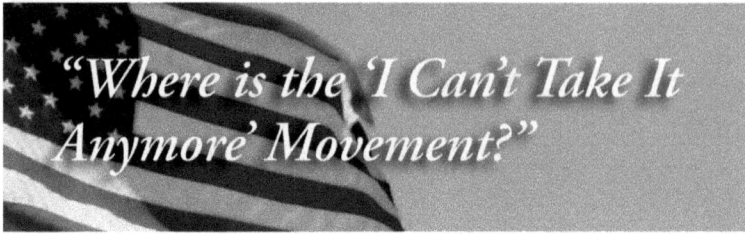

The question is??? Why are we making laws about laws faster than McDonalds can sell Big Macs…. We have a cause, a right, or a wrong, and we demand new laws to protect and ensure that only good will prevail. But as soon as a law is passed you can bet there is a law in waiting to better define the law in question. So we are better defining everything to the point of ??? Who cares??? Who cares about the laws. They are so complicated that they are ignored… until… somebody complains and sues… and sues… and sues… I have a right to sue is the birthchild of all the laws.

I was asked to sign a simple contract for airing a commercial. The rate and price was simple. I signed as agreed. They called back and said I had not signed the terms of acceptance. Ok… So I go look again at the four pages of fine print I was supposed to rubber stamp and trust them. It would cost me a pretty penny to have my attorney review and then get back to their attorney. I said shove it. Cancel the spot. In fact, it is insulting that they ask us to sign fine print without their paying for your attorney to review. Hello??? We abrogate our rights. Oh, by the way, they called back and said everything was ok. They would run the spot.

Our existence has been "fine printed." That is why the word "whatever" has become a philosophy of its own. Fine print is everywhere lurking in the shadows ready to hold you responsible… We need to be tortified or detorted or something. We are being torted to death by our own laws. We are being wronged by our laws. Admittedly we need laws…but is there a limit? Where is the "I Can't Take It Anymore" Movement???

Maybe it is time to move west again and farm my own land… say three to four acres… Get some ducks and a horse… and a gun… Like they did when they came over here from England. LOL.

What EVER (two words) happened to tort reform? Weren't we working on making frivolous or unfair lawsuits illegal? Lawsuits that were made easy by laws? Yes tort reform… Kinda got lost in all the international crisis attention and all the economic stagnation debate and all the political negative excitement. I mean really lost. Well, at least we have the Supreme Tort.

"Minority Rules"

We have freedom. We are a multicultural miracle. We have an economy engined by democracy with unlimited potential if we get out of the way.

We have taken the spirit of man and created a system where he can grow and gain regardless of his outer shell. In WWII we fought alongside our brothers from the human race, not of a race. Powerful. Ask any veteran of any war. Do you have the courage to actually ask someone who really knows? Or do we lack the courage to so honor them? Think about it. It is so much easier to watch a medal given to someone on TV… So much easier.

I grew up and we team members voted to see who of us would be captain of the football team. I didn't win. We took a count, and the person getting the majority of the votes won. Majority rules or something. It has worked all through life, for the most part. We didn't have to deal with the feelings of those who lost, much less mine.

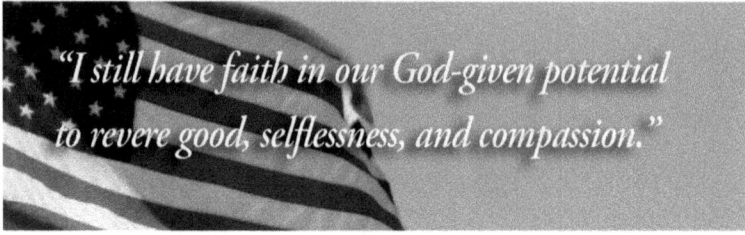

It seemed like a fair process. And life went on. Feelings were a natural byproduct of all decisions. Too Bad was ok. Suck it up. Be a man. It worked. Diversity was and is a blessing. An arrangement of flowers. Human blossoms. Oops, forgot to read the card… "Love God". Except we didn't open the card.

The race of race started with Martin Luther King's tragic murder. The nation shook with grief, anger, and resolve. Movements and laws pounded the establishment and there was no turning back. The problem lay with the majority who had some evolving and maturing to do. It is better now for many. But corruption, greed, and irresponsibility took the wind out of the sails and has left many sitting on the curb… Fatherless homes and jobless masses became the breeding ground for the new poverty. The new prison. And it is diverse. Diversity in crisis.

As the cries of despair rose so did the cries of every injustice. Now something new was going on and that was the emergence of powerful media access to pain. This is good… But the ensuing (pun intended) search for "who to sue" gave media more material, more news. Pretty soon every minor cause had found a pulpit. The voracious appetite of media for content consumed every local possibility for news. And we fed on it.

The new paradigm became feeling centric. You can't offend anyone became more important than you can't offend everyone. Repeat it. You can't offend anyone became more important than you can't offend everyone. On any given day a minority news flash became important. Incident after incident… in schools, in homes, at work. Every wrong became a right with two lawyers in tandem. The majority began to be excluded.

How can a politician cater to so many rights and wrongs, so many causes, without being vilified by even the smallest minority?

Enter the socialist democratic agendas with their infinite sensitivity to the minorities. Rants with ties on. The conservative shrinks. He wishes he were a minority so he would be defended. The majority has become the embattled minority. But I still have faith in our God-given potential to revere good, selflessness, and compassion.

I still believe the American dream of old where a handshake was a million times more efficient than fine print. Back then minority ruled as each individual contract had value. Our minorities deserve the same.

"Facecrook"

What would it be like to live without a face? Anyone we don't know has no face. For isn't it the first thing we seem to remember about another person, loved one or one not so loved??? We spend so much time looking at our face. When we brush our teeth first thing in the morning. When we are young we look for blemishes. When older for so many things, but often to privately observe our aging. We don't like to talk about our own faces, but we love to observe others. We put all kinds of stuff on our faces for all kinds of reasons. It seems as if our face is our most important possession. Our faces also contain our eyes through which we observe other faces. And through our eyes we can tell others that we care or that we don't. Amazing thing, faces... What would it be like without them?

I have my face in Facebook. I thought a lot about which picture would look best so others would always envision me that way. You know, like your best foot forward, except that it is my face. I makes me feel good to see my face looking good. That one picture... thank God...

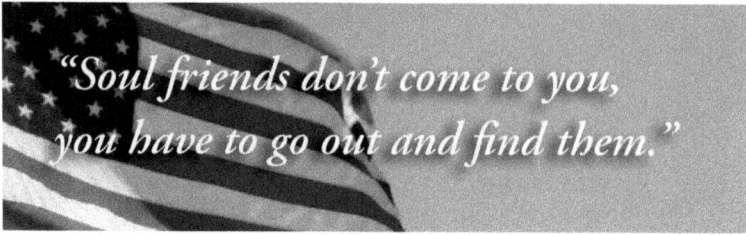

> *"Soul friends don't come to you,*
> *you have to go out and find them."*

Other people put their faces on my page or ask me to go look at theirs on their pages. Bet they also chose from many pictures. Now we all know what we look like. Whew… Sure makes things better. Amazing how everybody's face is different. Evolution is some miracle! Glad I don't look like a frog. Now I can share feelings and activities with my rapidly expanding universe of "face friends". Well… of course, I will only share those feelings that won't reveal too much…

Maybe there could be a thing called SOULBOOK, where very special friends could share who they really were. Friends who were not afraid to say what they really felt… What does a soul look like? Does it have a face? Qualities of a great soul would have to have humility, unselfishness, and a compassion to help others. That really rules out ego, titles, money, and the material. Well, that is just my feeling. I know the people I am comfortable with. How about you? Do they really make you feel comfortable??

SOULBOOK… They probably have one up in heaven. But I need it now! I want more friends to share my soul values with. Get the right team of friends where you can trust and act without a lot of debate or corporate doublespeak. How do you trust? Go through some tough times with another. Yes... Military for sure. Helping the poor together, yes. Or find a place where values are still black and white. Some churches, probably... Soul friends don't come to you, you have to go out and find them.

Our insecurities are the bane of our growth. They are our enemy. We worry way too much about what others may think of us. I say, "Too Bad." I have to save my soul and make something of my life. I want to be something meaningful to others. Get out of my way. "Too Bad." I will not let the obsession with faces steal (crook) my real identity. Nope, no FACECROOK you FACEBOOK. I GOT IT!!! Put the pictures of people I have helped in my SOULBOOK. And keep my face out of it.

"IPO"

Initially I wanted to make my ideas public. But who really cares about my ideas? Hello? Along comes social media. Never heard of such a thing. Now it is all they talk about. I walk down sidewalks and all passersby have their heads down as they text others with their ideas… We older folks just have to catch up. But my running days are over…

Social media??? What ever happened to the "cocktail party"??? Ok, we all know that an IPO is an Initial Public Offering. Stock market lingo for "get in first" and make a lot of money. Handy little acronym, IPO, to drop at cocktail parties or "hanging out" events??? Nothing like making quick money to make yourself stand out. Kinda gives you immediate status and something to talk about. Makes you a celebrity so you can wear sunglasses indoors…

Well let's talk about initial public offerings in more depth. How about the times one initially offered oneself to the public when a teenager? You know, like the first time you

dressed up for a dance. Nervous as a teen and now nervous as an investing adult. The public makes us honest. Publicity allows others to look more closely at us. It is looking for mistakes and for strength. Don't know if I really want to be publically offered.

I'm partied out. Do you get it? I'm Partied Out, or IPO. That is really the better acronym definition. We all try to do so many things so fast. Instant results based on instant data, demographics, statistics, polls, and opinions… In fact the latter is the most insidious criteria by which we try to make quick decisions. Other people's opinions are needed when we don't have an answer which is usually most often. Oh, we think we have the answer, but we really don't and the first opinions will carry significant weight… precedes the facts anyway. My wife sure has opinions and they are the first in the mix.

Well, next you have the morning news shows. I always start with "Morning Joe" to see which horse Mika and Joe beat to death… (though they really are good). After a work day the evening news refines what is important before I follow up into the wee hours on my iPad. Multitudes of opinions are the jigsaw puzzle we have to put together into something coherent so we can have our own opinion.

I am partied out on opinions. Yes, I'M PARTIED OUT!!!

Now I just want having my own opinion to be less difficult. I bet that if I had all my values sorted out, that if my values were rock solid I could use them to make most decisions and get on with getting on. So where do you turn to reshape values? That is the question we all have to face. Many just choose not to face it. Many just party on and waste life's precious time.

Distractions and pleasures abound that steal our initial public worth from us. Some are blessed with strong and demanding parents or friendships. I feel some are blessed by the cultural integrity of the military and some strong institutions. Maybe many are blessed by the Churches as long as unavoidable hypocrisies don't create the excuses we use to avoid them. I have worked through those all along and the reward has been worth the doubts and challenges to my spiritual journey.

Give it a try… Things are so much simpler. I'm partied out. I have no energy for the dither and multiplicities of opinions and "offerings". An Initial Public Offering is meaningless until it has stood the test of time. So are we…

"American Idol-atry"

What a wonderful "Live" show. Young people singing their hearts out in pursuit of fame and recognition and love...
I like all the "Live" shows as they are so much more real than all the other shows which are so expertly edited and formed to entertain us. Every nuance and sound is studied to be "just so" before being released to us to pretend as real. America's Got Talent, X-Factor, Dancing With The Stars, and so on... help us see stars being formed.. and they are live...!!! Well, sort of... Actually the NFL and NBA are more live.

As your stars are formed they morph into idols that we all can follow and dream about. They become idols to millions of followers. Of course, there are celebrity idols in movies. There are celebrity executives in business, and in every endeavor in life. The media turns them into idols depending on the fashions of the moment. Idols are born right in front of us. Thank God we have enough of them to give every one of us our own idol. American Idolatry is part

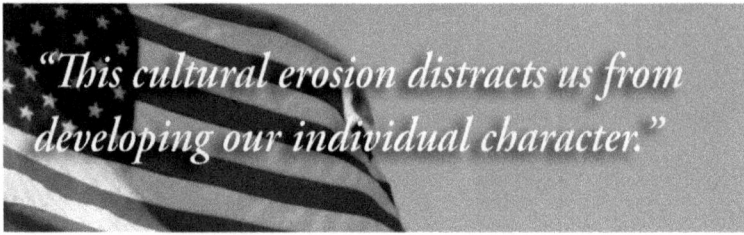

of our culture. Like having someone to love and admire when we are "in-between" relationships.

Idols are actually far away from us living their own lives. Moreover, we can still envy their fame and good fortune. Ok, maybe not envy, but certainly enjoy and share in their luck. Then we have the magazines and television to help us stay on top of their good luck… However, in not too long a time we will start to read about their human side. They begin to have problems. Our idols start to take on flaws when the lighting is no longer perfect…It doesn't matter. "Live" TV will once again give us new idols to fantasize about. Whew… started to worry.

You know, some really good idols have charities that they assist or create. Nice. I like these idols. I still like to read about all their love affairs and cars… And… the inevitable weight gain and… the inevitable drinking challenges. Oh well, being an idol ain't easy…

The problem is that the next step for an idol is that they become god-like. The word "idol" speaks of worship like in the ancient old days. This is dangerous territory.

When you start down the idol road and take your first nibble of this pleasure you give up a little of yourself. We all know about the perils of addictions. But this idolization has to be harmless??? Though when we love an idol are not we giving up a small part of our self? Is this the wasting of self??? Is self not a precious resource? Is self an endangered species? Should we not treat it with more care??? In an era of eco-everything why should we not be concerned about the wasting of our unique spirit? We exercise to protect our bodies. We watch calories to watch our weight. Why don't we watch our media input to protect our souls and values???

OMG, don't you love that acronym??? Texting and social media are adding so much new richness to our stale vocabulary. LOL, Laughing Out Loud. OMG, Oh My God. We are learning to "acronymize" (my word) almost anything. Abbreviating substance… LOL.

American idols are allowing us to minimize the significant. This cultural erosion distracts us from developing our individual character. This gives us the excuse to put off the creation of our own uniqueness which can only be defined by the values of integrity, honesty, humility, and compassion. How can we mean anything to anyone if we are not formed in these values?

OMG am I asking questions about God???!!! LOL.

"Just Call
1-800-I AM-UNHAPPY"

Just call 1-800-I AM-UNHAPPY and the personal assistance of a voice prompt will take you to several real people who will be able to expertly pass you on until you get a dial tone. LOL. Isn't that the way it is? It seems that every time we need help on something these days we are given a number to call. Even better, we are directed to a website where all questions have been anticipated and answers created so you never have to cause the expense of having to talk to a person.

Except they don't answer your question.

Then you scour the website for the contact access where you get to fill out another form ad nauseum. That is if you can find the contact info which is usually obscure and at the bottom in fine print. Ah… the zenith of customer service takes you to the bottom…

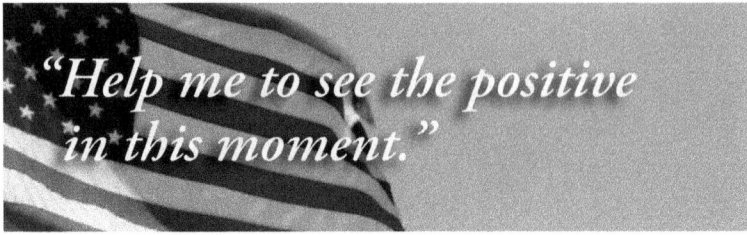

"Help me to see the positive in this moment."

Now back to our main subject, Just call 1-800-I AM-UNHAPPY. Yes, when I am unhappy, I need help, maybe just a little. I don't want to bother a friend with my minor troubles… but I want them to go away so I can be in control again. Nor do I want to compound the moment with being embarrassed by confessing my trouble to someone… I just need a number to call… Ok, except every number I call I get voice prompts. I watch television and there are endless commercials giving numbers to call to solve problems. Well, I should say, not really numbers, just access to voice prompts… I know, I can text or tweet friends…but do I really want them to know my weaknesses or personal frustrations??

Well, here we go again… you know me… I always start… "In the old days." LOL. Just kidding… I have learned, FINALLY, that the only number to call that works is 1-800-TRY-A PRAYER. I take a quiet moment, close my eyes… And pray. Maybe as simple as saying "Please dear God help me make this problem go away. Help me to see the positive in this moment. Help me find hope again. I just want to make others feel good again." Oops... maybe too personal to print. But who cares???... it works.

I know this is a radical right-wing approach to things. Yep, it's old fashioned and no longer endorsed by our schools or government. Only the outsiders do something like this. Only some minority. Only a few making noise that is insignificant. Of course, you get to see it on TV immediately as "breaking news". Prayer as "breaking news"... I love it. Not for me, nope. Not prayer. I prefer voice prompts... Just call 1-800-I AM-UNHAPPY. If you have the iPhone you can talk to "Siri" who will answer all your questions... if lost she will give you directions... if you need to find a restaurant in any city in the world she can get you the menu. I am sure if you are unhappy she will console you and recommend a distraction. Thank God for "Siri."

Oops, cell phone is ringing. Hello. It's 1-800-I AM-UNHAPPY asking me if I want to make a donation to their Social Security version, the UPSF... (Unhappy People Security Fund).

"The Blame Game"

I am guilty. I will take the blame. I will never do it again. It was stupid and I wasn't thinking. Really Dad, I didn't mean to hurt anyone. Can I pay you back? But, please don't take my driver's license away. Please. Mikey made me do it. This is the Blame Game. The most important rule of the game is to not blame yourself. Repeat after me, very important... I am not guilty. It is not my fault. Once you get past this hurdle you are home free. The sense and taste of freedom is like a gourmet meal. Ahhh... really good. It is so good to feel good again. After all it was not my fault.

But other people know what happened and it is important for them to know whose fault it really is. Ok, let me think who was around when it happened. Aha, that guy, Michael, was there and said the thing that triggered me. Yes, Mikey. Everyone must be told ASAP. I am on it. My "A" game... the blame game. Mikey is not very good at defense anyway. It's also fun watching the blame stick on someone else. Especially since that person "ain't" me. Yessssss! Whew, the

first part is done. Peace at last. I do feel a little bit guilty though… Mikey is a good guy. Maybe I should implicate Frankie to take some of the pressure off Mikey???

Now… Let's say that 30 years have passed. I have kinda worried about Mikey all that time. I kept it to myself but I really worried about what I may have done to Mikey. I wasn't fair… but… well… I sure got myself out of a jam. Thank God.

Yet, the look on Mikey's face still haunts me… especially at night. It's too late to blame someone else in the past. Damn, this doesn't feel right. Poor Mikey.

It seems that it is OK to blame someone else. Everyone does it these days. Go look at the news on TV. Look at those famous political commentators, much less the politicians themselves. Look at those senators standing up and blaming. The solution to solving problems is mired in the blame game. Wow. Blame the last administration. Blame the next administration. How did I get in this mess? Maybe I can blame them for making blaming so acceptable? Now that I am older and know more about life I see things a little differently. I have certainly seen all my friends make mistakes. I have seen a few do the right thing, usually unselfish, and I respect them for that.

You know, if I could do it all over again I would not have brought Mikey into it. I would have just said I did it and taken the heat. Would have been long gone and I could have done more with that energy saved. Yes, I had nobody to blame but myself.

How could I have known not to blame? Deep down inside I knew. But shhhhh, don't want anyone to hear... I knew it was really wrong and I made a choice. I made a bad choice. I am sorry Mikey. Will you forgive me?

"Debt or Prison"

A trillion dollars of debt! Now that is a figure I can work with. I can get my arms and brain wrapped around that one. Multiples of a trillion are now easier to manage. A trillion dollars, yessss!!! Debt is always something you want to reduce to zero. I am told the happiest people are the ones with no debt and who do not spend beyond their income. Those are the crazies out there who quietly manage and enjoy life. They never feel they are owed anything. Where in the world did they get such a misdirected notion??? Where??? Now back to the trillion. Just a thousand billion dollars. Let's see… if I give half of my $50,000 income to pay down my personal debt of a trillion dollars I will be able to borrow again in 400 million years. Ok, I up the payment to $250,000 a year and it will only take four million years. Ok, so we get 400 million people to pay $25K per trillion dollars of debt and??? It's all in the math. Hmmm, a trillion is bigger than I thought. I think none of us has any idea how large it really is… I don't think the government does either.

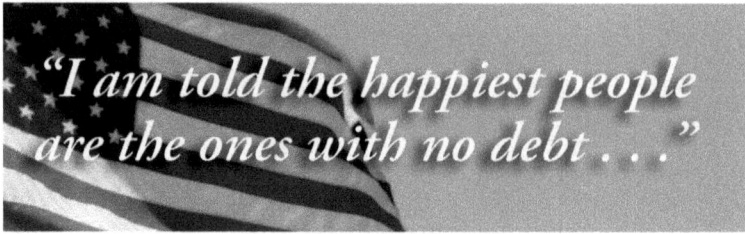

OK, math does not work. There is no logic to it. Let's pay it off in 10 years. One hundred billion a year will do it, not including interest, of course.

Now when I get in debt at the mini household level and my credit cards max out I am in trouble. No more discretionary buying, or should I call it "indiscretionary" buying?? No more going out. No more vacations. The predicament is very painful and embarrassing. I can't go out and have my card declined in public... Bad. How to escape the embarrassment? Drinking? With less money and cash??? I don't think so. Without my credit card I am nobody.

Debt used to be so fun. I was always able to stay ahead of it. Thought the government... Thought the government...

Future generations are at risk... but that is the future... not now. But wait, these are my kids and grandkids that my excess has put bull's-eyes on their foreheads. Their dollar will be worth much less. Bet a Big Mac will be $20.00.

That is prison. Debt or prison? Debtor's prison.

"Laughter"

WHY ARE YOU LAUGHING AT ME?

Why??? Are you making fun of me? Other people will see you laughing at me and will make fun of me. You are not nice. I am leaving. Ever heard that before? Don't laugh or I will stop writing. If you are laughing at me I don't have the confidence to ignore it. My self-image is at risk. But it is not at risk if I laugh at you and make fun of you. Laughter is so much fun if it is at someone else's expense. I love laughing. Can't wait to get together with my buddies and have good laughs. Feeling good from laughter is just the best! Jokes are great too, especially the ones which catch you off guard, that surprise you. Comedians like Jay Leno and the late night guys are wonderful as long as they stay clean... Wit is wonderful... British humor is dry and fiendishly funny most of the time. We are a country that has freedoms that allow us to laugh a lot more than others.. I bet freedom to laugh is in the Constitution somewhere... I have my rights, and one of them has to be a right to laugh whenever I want.

Did you catch the last part??? "Whenever I want."
Hmmm... That may be a problem on occasion. Because
when I want might not be when someone else wants. Or
they might not be able to see the humor that I see. What
do we do then? What happens if they make a wisecrack
back that they think is funny and I don't??? No longer is it
funny. Some people hate something that they do not think
is funny. Then they hate the person who tried to be funny.
Oops... Humor breeds the opposite??? Out of context is a
big problem with humor.

This week on television, media pundits have been going
at it really serious. Politics is ruining humor. These guys
are becoming sooo sensitive. I don't want to mention
which party... but they are becoming masterful at
creating contexts where they can take the humor out of
humor. They can laugh with a destructive glee... making
fun of an important figure gives them a power over the
entertainment of information. They take humor and forge
it into a new metal of combat. They wear coats and ties as
their uniform. They anchor cable, print, and network. My

only defense is my remote. I keep extra AA batteries more close by these days.

I make sure I have a drink at hand before I turn on the TV when I get off work. It loosens me up a little and makes it easier to laugh if something funny happens. I want to laugh more. National debt does not make me laugh. Poverty does not make me laugh. Chris Christie makes me laugh. Or should I say cringe at what he gets away with. He is making the truth funny. Now what would be really funny is to have someone skinny from the other side be funny.

All kidding aside it is time to laugh again and not be afraid to do so.

"Hate"

I really hate pistachio ice cream. I also hate any ice cream with mint or that is green. I love frogs. Girls hate frogs. I love vanilla swiss almond. Boy… that vanilla is the best. But, when you crunch on those chocolate covered almonds it is better than the best glass of wine or anything unmentionable.

I hate people who hate. I really hate to hate. I hate writing this. I am beginning to love to write, but I have been asked to do that.

Let's get back to hate. Hate feels good as it allows you to direct all your frustration on to something or someone. A quick cure for inaction? Sometimes we hate someone because we can't change them. Or… they won't listen. How can my wife listen when she is talking? We won't go there…

How did we learn to hate? When was the first time you ever hated something??? When I was a little boy I don't

think I hated anything. But soon my parents started telling me what to do. I started to not like that. Then when I got spanked. I didn't really hate because I knew I deserved it. It kind of molded me to think and act more appropriately. Then I became a teenager. I hated pimples. I hated feeling insecure. I hated pretending that I was not. In the Navy, they really got tough. You didn't get a chance to think for yourself. Then came Hell Week. I hated the cold. I hated the pain. I hated the exhaustion. Well, not really. I was proud and I was not alone. We were forged into men. I hated the politics in business. I never saw anything coming.

I never knew what hate really was until I got older. I never knew what it was until I started hearing others say how much they hated others. The wars were sure reasons to hate. Slavery was a sure reason to hate. Racism was something to hate. Bigotry was something to hate. Lying is something to hate. Selfishness is something to hate. Prejudice is something to hate. Prejudging is something to hate. There is too much hate to hate. I hate the way politics has evolved.

Finding fault is now a science. A blemish is a headline. A sin is covered up. Money makes truth go away. Talking points obscure realities. Makeup hides the pallor. It is no longer easy to see the truth. I hate that. I hate to keep going back to television… But this is the media where we can see and hear the damage of hate. I go to one cable station for one form of hate… I go to a network for another kind of hate. I go to another for international hate. Sublime hate. In-your-face hate. A restaurant of hate.

Maybe that is why the Food Channel is so popular. What's to hate? Nothing… as long as they don't visit pistachio ice cream restaurants…

"Despair is the Solution"

Don't despair. Wonderful phrase. Have you heard it before? It has to do with no hope. What is hope? Hope is just wishing something will happen. Sounds like both of them are kind of silly.

It is easy to say don't worry. Actually when you say don't worry the worrier gets more worried. Usually life provides the next interruption and there is something new to think about and the worry gets put back in at the end of the line. Don't worry, there will be something new to worry about. Now despair is much worse than worry, because despair means there is no solution and you really have something to worry about. Hey, it's not too separated from fear.

How do people historically deal with really bad circumstances, not just the worry ones??? Well, they believe there is something more to life than worry or a negative and defensive point of view. There is a choice each of us has to make. Life either has meaning or it has no meaning. If it

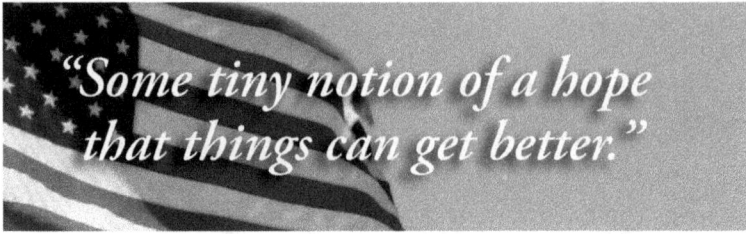

has no meaning then there is so much to worry about that it is total despair. Fruitless, worthless existence. Evil and good have no meaning. Nihilism. Nada. Go kill someone. It doesn't matter. Despair is the solution as no other action matters.

Suppose there is a thing called hope? The antithesis of despair. Then, maybe, life may have some meaning. Hope seems to energize the positive. Hope seems to provide strength when all seems bleak. Hope means that you believe something good can happen, no matter the moment. It means you have faith that something good will evolve. Hmmm…

A mother cares for her child like no other. Why? For her there's hope that good will come to her child. That if she guides with integrity and honesty that her child will survive and be happy. She commits her whole being to this notion with hope and faith. I think she knows what despair is. I think she abhors despair. Maybe despair is the engine of hope?

Kids today are being enabled by their video games and entertainment media to discard the notion of despair. There is always some form of instant gratification. A Big Mac is a few dollars away. A sugar-laced soda a dollar away. Escape through peer cliques offers tribal protection. Despair is more under control than ever. But, the looming job market is this giant wall facing them sooner than they think. The jobs that are available that aren't mind numbing require hard work, no cell phones or facebook, no infinite coffee breaks... Today, employment applications are e-mailed so they can claim the attempt at employment to be qualified for unemployment.

No despair when the system is played. So here we are, more confused than ever about life and how to game it.

I know a little about homeless shelters. Cathedrals of despair. You don't get in them until you bottom out. And you aren't in them until you admit you might have made some wrong choices, and then admit it was all your own responsibility.

The nadir of despair is looking in the mirror and seeing nothing. That is the moment of solution, abject despair. That is when one looks up and finds fragile hope. Some tiny notion of a hope that things can get better. Then you start to listen to the stories of others who are in various stages of hope morphing into Faith. Then you listen and start to hear, because for the first time in your life you are willing to listen… amazing "wow" stories of real conviction that a life is going to get on the right track and stay there. Tears abound from the families and victims. A "Praise the Lord" may be heard in the din… Despair has been their only solution. There is hope. We can be great. We can be strong. We can be right. We can be good. We can be free. Of despair.

"Avoidance"

Don't despair. Wonderful phrase. Used it in the last article. This is part two.

Don't despair, avoidance is the powerful management tool now available to you to control the unexpected. For only a $15.00 monthly charge this App, and the "Whatever App", can be yours. Complete protection from all unplanned discomfort. Download now. For $5.00 additional you can have our unlimited warranty that will reimburse you for any momentary disruption. Now available for iPhone... iPad version coming soon.

Whatever. This is the most powerful new shield from our teenagers to help us cope with any question posed to us at any moment. Just look at the floor for a moment and say "Whatever" as you pass by and achieve another avoidance victory. Teenagers have simplified avoidance methodology into one word. We owe them a lot. After all, they are only distilling the obvious as they watch adults do the same thing with exhausting articulations and excuses.

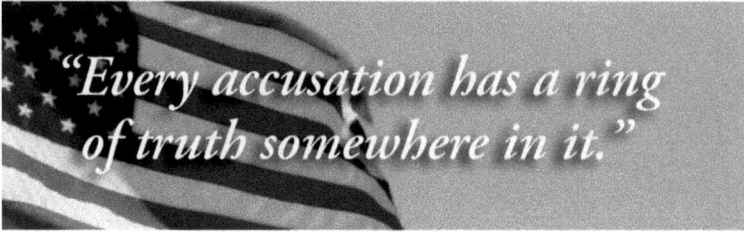

"Every accusation has a ring of truth somewhere in it."

Like… "Sorry I'm late"… "I couldn't pick up my phone"… "Ask your mom"… "Let me get back to you"… "That's on the agenda for next week"… (add your own… LOL). "WHATEVER!"

Then there is the attack meant for distraction. It is masterfully playing itself out in media and politics ad nauseum. Grab an airsickness bag when you turn on the TV. Which network do I trust, which ad do I trust, which reporter do I trust, which leader do I trust??? Every accusation has a ring of truth somewhere in it. The power and the undeniable evil of the half truth. But why??? Why are we allowing this??? Avoidance. We wish to avoid any discomfort. So we , yes we, let them get away with it. Accusing is deflecting. Accusing or counter-accusation is avoidance. Avoid the truth. Avoid values. Avoid tough love. "Whatever" is the solution. Avoidance is the dilution. It is diluting our culture, civilization, history, and self-respect.

Don't despair. Whatever.

"Entitled"

NOW THIS IS GOING TO BE THE MOST
DIFFICULT TO WRITE AND THE MOST
DIFFICULT TO UNDERSTAND. But you are entitled
to a full explanation of what is due to you. You should
never accept anything less than the truth. That is your
right. From your parents came the decision to gamble with
your existence and after that magical moment you were
entitled to your first breath. No one has a right to take that
away from you. Tell me if that is what you think. But more
importantly are you entitled to love??? I think so. What is
the point of life if you aren't entitled to love? Think about
it. You have to make some decisions at some time in your
life. Think about it. What has value and what does not?

I think we think we are entitled to value. Well, we get
to make choices on what to buy based on value. We are
entitled to that right. The right to purchase what we want,
when we want… right? We are entitled to love when we
want. Right? Are we entitled to good behavior on the part

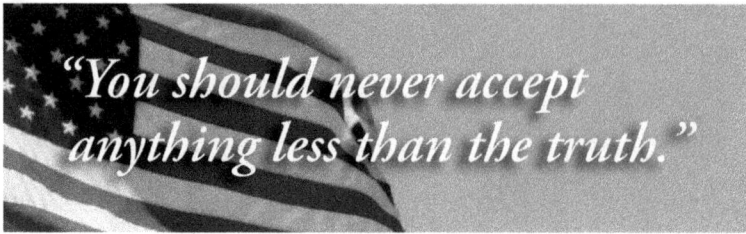

of others??? Are others entitled for us to act responsibly and with compassion? A lot to think about.

Are bad guys entitled to justice? Are nice Democrats and nice Republicans entitled to a country safe from harm and debt? If I am rich am I entitled to respect? If I am poor am I entitled to respect and compassion? If my neighborhood has been invaded by crack am I entitled to a way out? Maybe... Years ago, before you were born, the concept of entitlement was seldom heard as everyone was so busy working and helping one another. Hands were held and hope was the force that launched our amazing nation. Immigrants from England, Ireland, France, Italy, and Spain came on boats of all sorts. Nothing like today. Conditions were marginal to say the least. Ellis Island was full of our fathers like deer in the headlights. They expected nothing. The only thing they felt entitled to was freedom from discrimination. That is what the United States offered to those wishing to gamble their pasts and plights. Only hope. Entitled to hope.

WWI and WWII were fought as we felt we were entitled to freedom. Look at every cemetery from Normandy to Arlington. Seas of white freedom crosses. They were entitled to their crosses. They are entitled to our prayers and gratitude.

Whatever happened to our great country? Yes, there has been selfishness and greed and crime that created the need for more laws. Laws require millions of people to obey and as many to interpret and enforce. Bureaucracies of enforcement and code grew under the radar screen. Paperwork justifying paperwork became a cancer. Insurances that insured everything metastasized. Groups of interest unified and these unions became monoliths where members now became managed rather than served. Somewhere entitlement became the vision of this new culture. Be lucky enough to work for a public bureaucracy and you have pensions and insurances second to none. Special interests protecting special interests. The politics of survival has become entitlement.

In this new world order of entitlement our young are just expecting more.

Our culture is one of instant gratification. Media, video, headphones, and iPhones have become the Pavlovian conditioning elements of entitlement. With jobs scarce and debt responsibilities ignored at both the personal and national level, chaos is near. Kids expect money. The next generation expects to be paid more for less. We oblige and nurture the "entitled"... While they text one another... I am entitled to breathe, love, and to be entitled. If so, then the end is near.

"Wisdom From Ignorance"

NOW THIS IS GOING TO BE THE EASIEST TO WRITE COMPARED TO THE LAST ONE. LOL

Which comes first? The wisdom or the ignorance?

Did you ever think you have to be wise to be ignorant? Isn't it not fun when you say you know something and are proven wrong? Most of the time in our minds we have strong feelings about something and disagree with the person talking but keep quiet. And… in the end… are we glad we did because we found out we were wrong…? Or at least sufficiently unenlightened??

My fabulous dad used to say: "Chris, you don't learn anything when you are talking"… OK Dad… whatever… oops… 60 years later he was right. Boy, was I stupid.

There is so much knowledge out there if we would just read and listen. It would be really wise to do so. And even the ignorant can just Google and find fact. Google is beyond comprehension. It is almost like talking to God. Where else

> *"Challenge their idealistic spirit without compromise."*

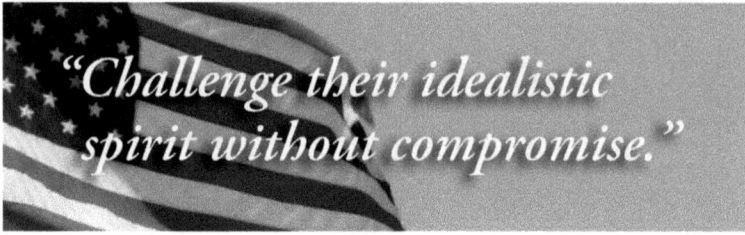

can you find fact without the subtle bias of newspaper and commentator editorials? Professed media professionalism has become the dither between ads. LOL

But we don't like to learn from history. We act ignorant that things have happened; wars have been fought, and we stumble forward with speeches professing solutions and outcomes without commitment. Inaction is our sword. But the enemies, and yes, hello, there are enemies, know how dull it is.

In our newfound genius we ignore the past and celebrate our sophistication and degrees and act as if utopia is attainable. With the right bureaucracy fairness will be administered. Sounds great, but who is listening to the past?

So does wisdom come from ignorance? If you are ignorant but listen, are you wise??? Hmmm...???

After college and the Navy and many years in business I found that the most brilliant people came from little or no formal education. They had to work for everything they got. They often worked to pay for their college and never lost that work ethic. Work means giving up a lot of your "private time." But work teaches about life, degrees don't. Colleges don't teach values other than the number kind. How can some of the most successful businesses be created or run by those without formal education?

Is selflessness taught in college? Is self-sacrifice taught in college? In business and the military, more wisdom is taught because you have to listen or pay a price. Here reality is taught, not theorized about.

Oops, I bet eyebrows are rising. Let's take education head on. Education is all about righting the wrong of ignorance. Right?

I think universities could be bastions of higher wisdom if they would put their feet back on the ground, look each student straight in the eye and proclaim they will not let them down. That they will prepare them for the combat of life. That they will teach more about how things work and fail by using more real people to give witness even if their grammar and accent is not comforting. And damn it, teach them that there is right and wrong and that there is a price to be paid for not listening. Teach black and white before you teach grey. Teach integrity, not tenure. Prudence not pension. Challenge their idealistic spirit without compromise. That you cannot have solar dreams without mud on your boots. That you cannot have freedom without blood on your hands.

Don't be ignorant about wisdom. Listen to your fathers and forefathers.

"Bang Bang"

BANG BANG, you almost shot me down. Great song by a great singer during great times, the 60's. Our society was in transition on so many fronts. Looking back now it was a period so rich in music from the Beatles to Beach Boys to Sonny & Cher… the list is endless. The world was in turmoil with the war in Vietnam. Lapels and pants for men were narrow (and it is headed back there today). It seems like a miracle that we have survived all that has transpired since then, much less since WWII.

Miracle is a word that suggests some amazing, almost impossible feat. It is a word that we use when we describe when something really fortuitous, something really good happens to someone. "It must be a miracle that Vickie was not killed by the car that ran the red light". You know what I mean. Or "It was a miracle I made it back from Afghanistan alive." Or "It was a miracle that Sally's baby survived…"

> *"It is a miracle in its own right that joy is part of the mix of existence."*

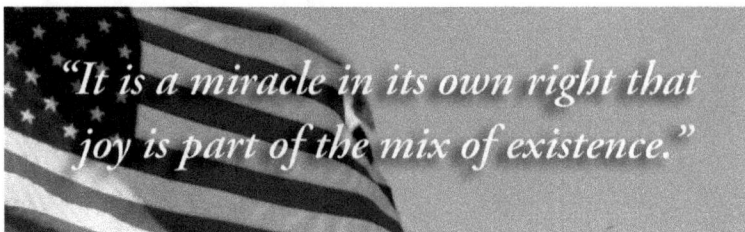

Miracles? Science is a miracle. Can we believe the mathematics that works from science? Or physics or chemistry or medicine? Think about all the things that you can characterize as a "miracle." I think we all have used the word to describe something that cannot be explained. Usually a miracle is something good.

Have we ever heard someone say that a murder or a disaster was a miracle? I really feel that the birth of a child is a miracle to behold. In fact, most of us marvel at the birth of most anything… puppies, kittens, calves, foals… and on and on. Why is it that we cherish and marvel at that moment?

Is there not something so special and miraculous about it? A birth is a gift to life. We cradle, caress, protect and love anything just born. The most special of all things we experience while alive on planet Earth.

Planet Earth is a miracle of sorts. I had the blessing to play a small part in our space program. Man flung man into orbit in Gemini and Apollo spacecraft where they took the most amazing pictures of planet Earth. Look how dead the moon is. Look how alive Earth is. The blue of the oceans, the white of the weather, the brown and green of the land. Amazing. What a miracle.

Well.. science and mathematics got our astronauts back safely to Earth (...with a little help from my buddies.) There was joy on the carrier; there was joy in the nation. Akin to the joy of birth or the saving of a life. You know, let's look at joy for a moment. Is it not the very best of feelings? Where does it come from? It is a miracle in its own right that joy is part of the mix of existence.

Well, there is limited space allowed here by the newspaper to explore miracles further so I will get to the point... Sort of... LOL. Look how far man has come in the last 2,000 years AD.

Look how far man has grown in the last 10,000 years. Well... except that he has not lost his penchant for war, lust, greed, evil, and self-centeredness...

That aside, it is amazing. Just think that the ignorant fire starter caveman now holds an iPad!! Miracle?

What I like better is that he evolved from some ape animal which evolved from some simple cell form of life which happened when some live dust particles from a billion light years away created our solar system.

What I like best of all with this whole interpretation of our miraculous existence is that it all started with a bang, a really big bang. Miracle. That explains it all. But I just don't accept it. There had to be a bang bang, a first bang before the bang created by something that had energy and design. Otherwise nothing makes sense. Science makes no sense unless there was a bang bang miracle. Thank God for bangs.

"Rights Anonymous"

What right do I have to be right? What are the rights of the right? Does someone else have to be wrong for me to be right? Do I have to be quiet or do I have my rights? Is to disagree a right or is it a wrong? Help me. I am so confused about what is right.

Well, first of all, being wrong is not right. Let's repeat it… "being wrong is not right". There are several types of wrongs. One, the innocent mistake that is just wrong and harms nothing. Simple wrong that we dismiss and forgive. No one needs to know and we learn. Then, more importantly, the wrong we know is not a mistake because we knew it was wrong beforehand and did it anyway. Bet this one affected someone else… like in 95% of the time… ok, well… 100% of the time. Damage done, but don't think about it and move on. There are plenty of excuses available.

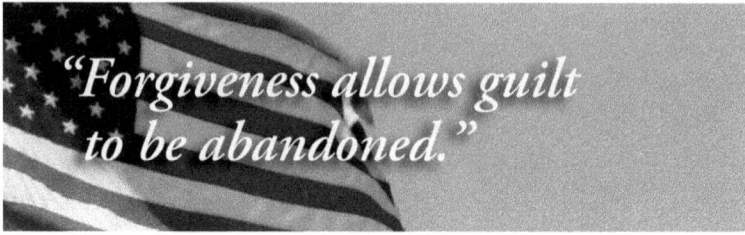

"Forgiveness allows guilt to be abandoned."

What right do we have to be wrong? None, absolutely none. If we had listened when told what was right and wrong from the beginning, wrong would have been less desirable. But no, we, us little we's...are self justified and unassailable. Ego, greed, lust, pride, envy, etc. are embraced and forgiven as necessary journeys...They are even celebrated in the gossip magazines.

Ok, now a big leap into this war of rights and wrongs, and... their rights. For instance, in the news these days is the predator. What he did is wrong, horribly wrong. There is no excuse for this behavior. Let justice take its course. What right did he have to be wrong? None. Absolutely none.

How can he right his wrong? By being honest with himself and us and apologizing for his wrong. By asking for forgiveness. We are capable of listening to this plea. But what about the wrongs done to those who did the wrong? Ghastly consideration. But, life does go on and builds from its pain and chaos. Forgiveness becomes the only weapon against all hidden, traumatic hurt. Forgiveness allows guilt to be abandoned. Forgiveness allows the scar tissue to form stronger upon the will and determination of the innocent victim. One can stand tall again as can the military veteran who has seen the unseeable.

Pillars of society can emerge from the pain of this chaos to lead us and our children down roads of right. Of right only. There is a war to be fought against the rights of the wrong. Who can lead if not all of us? Who can be demonstrably vocal against the wrongs in every moment? Who can see the wrong better than those who have been wronged? Let the wronged lead the right back to our rights!

"We have our rights!" is the cry of the masses. Is it not time that we all came back together and agreed upon what is right and wrong? We are getting nowhere as we have discarded our traditions and moral roots.

Democrats and Republicans dither over legalities and interpretations. They send the message that there is nothing right and wrong. They are wrong to claim to be right. It hurts.

"Too Bad"

Somebody said "Too Bad" to me once and it hurt my feelings… I can't remember how young I was. Maybe my Dad said it when I wanted to take the car out when I was 15. Chris, NO… But Dad…??? Please?… No! You are not nice!… "TOO BAD!" When you are a kid there is something final about a "TOO BAD."

These days you have to be very careful what you say around anyone and everyone. There are so many groups, causes, constituencies, and whatever that have emphatically defined their boundaries, borders, and bruises… I dare not even mention one for fear of being accused of being an enemy or selfish or antagonistic or anti their "just" position.

As you read a paper these days someone is accusing someone of terrible thinking or deeds. It is all about accusing. When you accuse the other person is forced on the defensive and will appear partially defeated. Shrewd tactics. Even better is to wage a silent whisper campaign

> *"How can you be you if you can no longer say no?"*

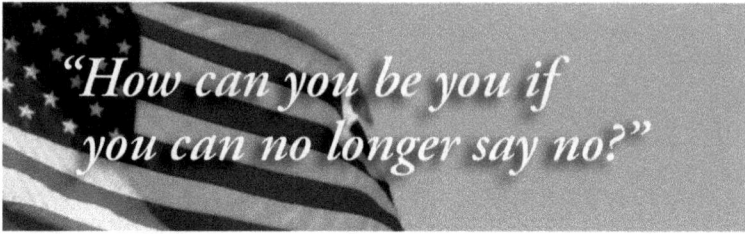

behind someone's back. By the time they find out the damage is done.

I think we should rename all causes and parties to one name. How about renaming the Republican Party to the IDP, the I Disagree Party.

How about renaming the Democratic Party to the IDP, the I Disagree Party.

How about renaming the Occupy Wall Street Movement to the IDM, the I Disagree Movement.

In fact we could do this to most every cause or movement where both sides are vehement. It would simplify things and the evening news could move on to trying to find its roots in truth, good, and constructive news. Let's report more good. Let's focus on collaborative solutions, not boring disagreement. Let's take the talking heads off our TV screens until they can agree.

I know that is a little harsh. I know that some of you disagree and are hitting the delete button. Aw shucks. What do I do? I think I say "TOO BAD" and get on with getting on.

Now we can write letters to the editor. Oh, and by the way, how about all the editors coming up with hair splitting logic that helps us wade through the sea of disagreement discourse? Most only offer politically correct "observations" or opinions. You know, this fear of hurting someone else's feelings has gotten out of hand. Now... do I hear a faint "Amen" out there???

We have become obsessed with what others think of us. We even think we know what others are thinking about us! We have become a culture of chameleons adapting to the perceived feelings of others! We have given up our unique identities by constantly being on the defensive in fear of criticism or unflattering opinion.

Again, are there not values or rights or wrongs that we stand for? Is there no longer anything unequivocal? How can you be you if you can no longer say no? How can you be you if you let your kid use the video game rather than throwing the ball with you outside??

"NO" has to be taken out of the dictionary and put back into our vocabulary.

"NO" defines you. Objections are to be welcomed with a "TOO BAD." Too Bad can free one from the tyranny of the feelings and opinions of others. Why do we think we need everybody to like us? Why are we glued to our cell phones while missing the clouds and stars above??? Why can't we say what is right reflexively? Too Bad if they disagree. Too Bad. I wanted to write something that hurt some feelings so I could say "TOO BAD". But if you agree with me then I can't say it. Maybe, I just want us to agree that disagreeing has gotten out of hand. Agree or disagree? Can you help?

"Who Were You Meant To Be?"

I was born in Bronxville. I didn't have a clue. Clueless in Louisville. Clueless in St. Louis. Clueless in New Haven. Clueless in Little Creek. Clueless in New York, Clueless in Los Angeles... And then... Something happened...

As we start our life journey on planet Earth we see grand things and grand people. Things that touch our unique child self. Let's see...there was Walt Disney, Bambi, Roy Rogers, the Lone Ranger, Flash Gordon, Jacques Cousteau, and of course very special for me "The Snow Goose" by Paul Gallico/Herbert Marshall. In our childhood we absorb all that amazement around us. I can't keep up with all that kids and teens have to pick from today. In my day it was all good and wholesome. Today it is a slurry of borderline amusement with brilliant new Disney, 3-D, and softened innuendos of permissive evil... Scary. How to make the right choices? Sneak under the covers with your iPhone

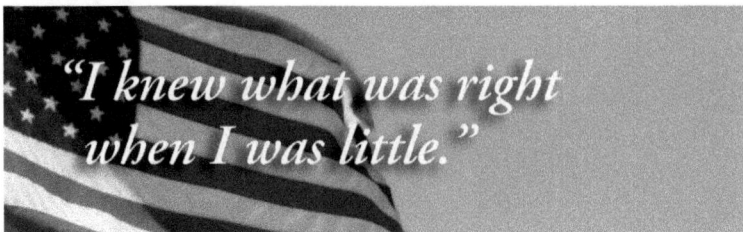

and see the world. Navy not needed. Wow! The world is a feast of visible paths to glory and fame. Cars, clothes, fashion, money. Get enough and everyone will think that you… Yes little old you, are really something. Looking the part is the most important first goal. Watch others to see what they look like to ensure that you look right. Then step out and stand tall. Except that someone else just got a new car and a big house and is sending their kids to a better school and just took a really amazing vacation.

Pressure, more pressure to be who I was meant to be. Well, at least I am still really good at my chosen sport or hobby. Everyone knows. That is good. It is important that others think that I am really good. Oops, really good? What does that really mean? I had better think a little more about it. Well…who do I really admire? My friends who have the most? Or… Maybe that guy down the street who is really struggling but keeps giving stuff away to people in need? I don't get it. Why do I secretly admire him? Why?

Why worry, go back to the TV or text my friends and I will feel good again. In fact this social network world has answered all my misgivings as I am "in the loop" and making things happen. Well at least in the social network of reality…

Yet, being quite honest.. there are insecurities that I keep pretty well hidden. They bug me. And I can remain ignorant about many things while able to hide it. I also see a lot of hypocrisy that I can look away from. Hey, even churches turn me off with their rules, rituals, and inconsistencies. I got it… Life is pretty much folly. It must just be about entertainment and avoiding discomfort at all costs. Yep, that's it.

But now I am really confused. Come on. Who were you really meant to be?

I have to knock down these superficial walls, my excuses that keep me from resonating with life, that keep me from resonating with truth, that keep me from resonating with good. I knew what was right when I was little. I want to be that way again. I want to be me.

The darndest thing is that I feel best when I am helping someone else. I have tried all the foods of life. They all lead different places and many into pain or guilt that is hard to digest. But there is one path that works. That path is helping others. Period. I am tired of trying to be something.

I can't look at me unless I am in a hurry to get on with helping thee.

I don't want my eulogy to say he liked his cars, he liked his dogs, he liked his friends. Life has nothing to do with what you like. It has only to do with who
you helped.

Let them talk. Who were you meant to be? Anonymous and good. That's all folks.

"Failing Schools"

"Our schools are failing." We politicians like to banter this one around a lot. Do the rich have better schools than the poor? Has more money been poured into the poor schools? Do teachers in poor schools teach better than teachers in the rich schools? Charter schools. Private schools. Religious schools. Home study. Forget-it schools…Good colleges, bad colleges. Good teachers, bad teachers. Tenure. Unions. HELP. No child left ahead. No teacher left behind. Program after program. Vision after vision. Bureaucratic mazes. Administrative mazes. I can't imagine the changing paperwork and online filing protocols.

Now if you really want to complain about schools then gimme 50 (pushups). Which came first, the student or the teacher? Or the union? Or the bureaucracy?

How about we change the chapter title to Failing Neighborhoods? Or how about to Failing Parents? Or how about to "Why Did my Father Disappear?"

"Which came first, the student or the teacher?"

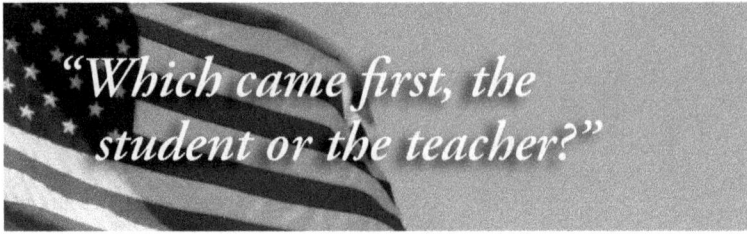

Yes our government has complicated the mess. But more importantly we have complicated the mess. The erosion of the family unit is more egregious than any other factor. How does a kid pay attention when he lives in a world of disrespect? How does a kid pay attention when his parents are addicts? How does a kid pay attention when his parents are selfish? How does a teacher know when a kid is hurting or thinking about something that is not fair or right that he brings to school every day??

We have let our values be trodden down by critics. We have let our values be weakened by the sensitivities of the overly sensitive. We have let our values be trodden down by our own insecurity. We are insecure because our values are not strong. Because we really don't believe in our values. Hello? Wake up. It is us.

We could blame it on social injustice and poverty. But what about those thousands of stories like Condaleezza Rice or our President? Humble backgrounds from parents who worked multiple jobs and raised kids who got somewhere.

They all refer back to the love and example of parenting. Money solves none of these problems if the father isn't there at night. And if the father doesn't have some rock solid values. Mom's too. We need a national debate and dialogue on values and where we came from.

Why have we put blackface on churches? Yes, denomination has become a wall for many. Rules and regulations which we abhorred as teenagers are institutionalized in denomination. More rules so we rebelled and left because we were not "comfortable." Maybe the discomfort was essential to grow? Why do they say "no pain, no gain?" Why do we have the best military? Because we train. (PS… I know.)

We have to come together somehow if we want anything short of self-destruction. Let's solve the debt problem and get back to making family the most important thing we focus on. The best students come from the best families. The best families are not the ones with the most cars or the biggest houses. The best families come from the best mom and dad who are strict as they know the value of values.

Failing schools? Who are we kidding? Give me a C - not a pass or fail.

"Gimme 50"

"Can you spare a dime?" over time became "Can you spare a 5?" Just 5 dollars so I can get a meal today. Standing at an intersection these days may be a homeless person with his hand and pride out. We don't like to look them in the eye. We hope that the light stays green so we don't have to stop right next to him. Maybe we pull over a lane to avoid the decision. And... most likely he is a fraud and part of a team that dresses up daily in their worst to play on our diminished compassions. Maybe...??? Oh what the heck... what's a $5?

Now of course if I were driving along a Hurricane Isaac-ravaged Plaquemines Parish street and someone had their hand out...? What about being in Haiti with all the outstretched eyes? What do we do with all the gimmees? What about the picture in the NY Times of the disfigured child and the website that can so easily be accessed? Gimme less pictures of pain.

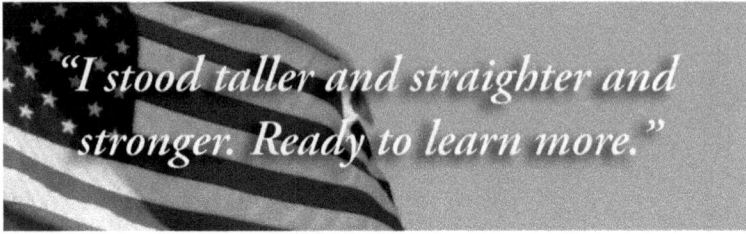

We are saved by media which now assaults us with tragedy after tragedy from Columbine to Damascus. So many injustices and needs that we are overloaded and can retreat without conscience to our safe rooms and ear buds. Jersey Shore and the Kardashians seem much more real. Their pain solicits my compassion too. Yeah, sure…

OK. Gimme 50. Gimme 50 real. No way. No way… unless… It's Christmas and it's the right cause… Or maybe to my needy politician…

Let me tell you what 50 real really is. It's 50 pushups. When I first heard it barked at me I said are you NUTS? It immediately became 100. And this monster Instructor (LTJG Hawes) stood over me until I accomplished 50, back bowing, arms on fire. One learns real fast. That is 50 real. If you don't do something right there is an expected, instant punishment. Or let's now call it discipline that will yield disciplined behavior. I was learning so many new ways to behave and act because I knew what 50 real were and how quickly they were meted out. After six months I had learned exactly what they wanted to me to learn... I stood taller and straighter and stronger. Ready to learn more.

Learning is all too often expected to be effort free. Teen agers expect it to be. Parents are reluctant to demand a 50 real every time their child chooses to ignore guidance. No pain, no gain kids. Families with substance have values that are taught and taught and taught. Punishments for disobeying are just expected. Strong men can remember back with pride how their dads trained them. The stricter the stronger in the end. I am proud of my dad that he made rules. I am proud of my dad that he reeked with values. Lucky or blessed??? I thank God.

Can you spare a dime? Yes I can. Can you gimme $5? Sure. Can you loan me $100? Yep. Because my eyes know truth. I have had values pounded into me by life. My eyes can tell me if you are playing with truth. My eyes are connected to my heart. My eyes are smarter than yours... or at least 100 gimme 50's smarter...

"The Morality Penalty"

Morality is a word you don't want to use these days except in privacy. Best be careful or you could be labeled. It takes a pretty confident person who is not afraid of being tossed into a radical group's label. If you are immoral you stand a better chance of being excused from scrutiny. You can be forgiven for being immoral, but not for being moral these days. Funny twist in semantics, or is it?

Funny, really funny how you had better posture yourself if you wish to say something moral. Or even describe some moral person in a positive light. Of course, there is moral, and then again there is moral.

Which makes you more comfortable? Funny. Ok, there is contemporary moral and then there is that Biblical kind of moral. The latter is really a problem these days. They want everything to be so black and white and prudish.

So let's examine easy moral. Or relatively easy moral. That is the kind where you ask your friend, one who you really

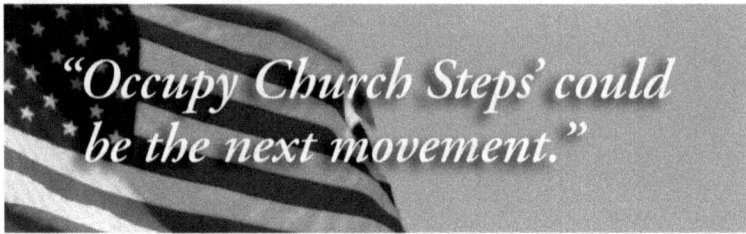

trust, if something is truly moral. Like if you really love someone who is already taken... but is not happy. Getting right to the point? You don't want to do anything immoral so you need the advice of a friend. The friend says don't worry if you both love each other. See? Easy.

Let's jump to the half-truth. Now this is the most used act in all of mankind. We use half-truths to protect the other person from the truth. Well, actually it saves us the embarrassment of being criticized for hurting someone with the truth.

Moral or immoral? Or self-serving? Or self-inflicting?

Most of what we see on television and in movies these days really obscures what is right and wrong under the guise of entertainment... Notice how taboos have slowly been evolving into treats? Science fiction used to be simple and romantic... Buster & Dale?? Now, OMG, zombies on planets, and invading monsters zapping our cities! No morals that I can see except when the hero briefly kisses the heroine on the cheek before killing the next drone robot. Of course, afterwards is the full passionate embrace alluding to more to come.

Now, I have avoided bringing in the other offensive buzz word, "values", because everyone defines their values differently. Try and get a majority to agree. So many contested values and interest groups that uniting eludes the most seasoned academia, politicians, and leaders.

Now clergy have a better spin on values and morality, but they have been diluted by denomination and spiritual discrimination. They have to watch their steps as their churches could be picketed for making too much of an issue out of morality. "Occupy Church Steps" could be the next movement. A real publicity penalty for trying to espouse values.

Why should you have to pay a penalty for trying to be good? You don't if you don't care what other people say. You don't if you believe in your beliefs.

In WWII we fought and died for our beliefs. I think the same can be said for Korea, Vietnam, Iraq, and Afghanistan... And whatever is next. Our beliefs were about freedom and values and moralities. Ask anyone who served.

Let's all think back on our lives and the good decisions and the bad decisions. I wish I had made a few less bad decisions.

I wish I knew a little more about values and people earlier. I would have spent more time listening to more people with values. I wish I had kept my grip on moralities and said no to myself more often. It is all so silly.

Who can cast the first stone? Everyone is criticizing everyone. The politics of criticism. Yuck.

Do you have to put yourself on a Cross to be good?

"Reflections Of A Black Teacher"

I have a friend who is a teacher. He is black too. Or should I say I have a friend who is black and happens to be a teacher. I have other black friends. Or should I just say I have friends? I have no Muslim friends. Why should having friends be complicated? Now this friend is peculiar as he should be writing a book I want entitled "Reflections of A Black Teacher." But he won't because he is too insecure. Not, "not ready," just insecure. He and I have traded e-mails regarding what I have been writing and his responses come from some other world. Really sensitive and insightful. But they are coming from his perspective. I did not grow up black, so he talks and thinks with different metaphors and images. It is like a different language.

We all grow up in our own worlds and many never see the world or life from any other perspective much distant

> *"He knows that values are the only way out, that values must be taught with strictness."*

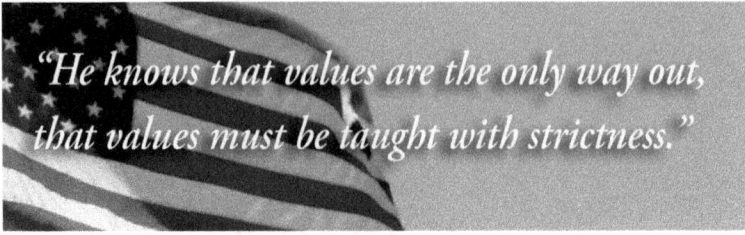

from our self-centered one. Being a teacher is not easy and certainly is politically charged these days. Being a black teacher adds another dimension of double political correctness. I want my friend to get off his posterior and write the book that he already has written.

We students, teachers, administrators, politicians, and general populace could use a personal journey through the maze of feelings experienced in his journey. Celebrities get to tell all. Why can't we? Are we less boring ??? Sometimes I want to respond to his musings that he is a reverse racist by all too often casting observations through a race tinted lens. Hey, but when am I not judging through my establishment eyes? Like all the time. I have been in the military where there really is no color. Who cares what the color of the guy next to you is when he may be the one who saves your life by taking your bullet? I can think that my friend has been in an administrative combat zone, where the bureaucracy of education often protects the weak at the expense of the brave. Where a union might have it backwards. Where a school board might be lost in correctness. Suppose you had to stand up in front of a school board and just be "not" black?

Now there is the world of the student who comes from the perfect parents without any bias. That comes from a loving mother and father who embrace and guide her with assurance and discipline. Yes, this is the norm. Well... Except that many fathers are no-show or never-showed guys. Then there is poverty. Then there is the entitlement mindset parent. Does the teacher have any idea of what healing might be needed? Of what bias the kid brings to the classroom? We do not have a lens into their minds or baggage. A really smart teacher knows and deals with this daily. He knows that values are the only way out, that values must be taught with strictness. Painful but necessary. Not necessary but absolutely essential. But it is not politically correct to do so.

Values are associated with religion. Religion is a bias. Religion is an imposition on the freedom of thinking. Game over. A sophisticated and caring teacher walks the career-ending tightrope as they try to impart more than just the schoolbook to their class. Sneak in a little manners. Sneak in a little unselfishness story. Sneak in a little success story. Sneak in a little story of hope. Sneak in an Olympian's success where with hard, impossible work miracles do exist.

I want my buddy to write his "Reflections of a Black Teacher".

That is why this white old man wrote this.

"Red Light District"

I was at a red light last night, stopped of course... And said to myself... Hmmm... This is funny... Why is everybody next to me and across from me stopped?? Oh, yes, it is the red light. It is just black and white. The red light, that is. Black and white. Simple, no argument. On red I don't go if I don't want to damage my beautiful car with someone crashing into it. Hmm.. Black and white. Traffic rules. So I wait until green, look right and left and go without a scratch.

Why is it that these simple rules are so easily followed by us surging masses? Because we know what the consequences will be. This is the Red Light District. Where danger abounds for the foolhardy and self-appointed egos. I am in charge. I am in control. Except at the red light.

Well, you gotta know where I am going... Capiche?

There are 10 ancient rules written on some dusty scrolls that I can't directly refer to because of political correctness.

You know, those silly rules about killing, stealing, and other forms of irrational behavior.

Why does a red light have to be hanging on some pole at an intersection to help us not hurt ourselves? You know, in the old days, for me the 50's and 60's, mom and dad laid down the laws. Hey, my parents loved me, well... at least what they hoped I could be... So I pretty much followed their rules. And lo and behold...whenever I went through their red lights I got in trouble. Funny, how could they be right and I be wrong? When I was a teenager I had right and wrong all figured out... and my parents were just wrong about things. Until I discovered otherwise...

What was cool about the Navy was that there were so many rules. So many "red lights". You can be sure you paid a price when you broke them. Now in the SEAL training if you so much as winked it was an extra 50-100 pushups or a dip in the icy ocean and rolling in the sand and then some run up a stupid sand dune. You know what? You learned fast or failed. Failure sucks.

Not an option. There was this swim buddy rule. Never get more than six feet apart. Run this red light and your next swim is with a six foot hawser (4" thick rope) around your necks. Hey, I now just love swimming close. I just do not understand all the idiots on dive boats when told to pair up, head their own merry way.

Red light? Black and white? Nope. Once again we have taken the liberty to take all that is black and white, or a red light, and turn it into grey so there is no decision to be made. All is now permissible as long as it is debatable...

A handshake used to be a man's word. Today, a man's word is his attorney. Just call 1-800-I AM-UNHAPPY and the personal assistance of a voice prompt will take you to several real people who will be able to expertly pass you on until you get a dial tone. LOL. Isn't that the way it is?

Red light, green light... a game we used to play as kids. It was so much fun to follow the simple rules. Today... run the yellow and don't look back... and see the camera in your rear view mirror and worry for a week if the other bureaucracy will mail you a ticket.

Today the red light is the only red light we don't run. And we are blessed with single parents struggling to make it while we import all the drugs we can... Enough to feed the need for human disappointment in spite of the valiant efforts of interdiction forces, good guys putting their lives on the line.

When will we be ignoring the Black & White and have consequences again? Why don't we treat our bodies and souls like we do our cars? Have we turned our own neighborhoods into Red Light Districts? Gotta go... Green light...

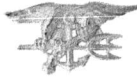

"Country Music"

Country music is so darn good and I have ignored it all my life. After all… it wasn't city… it was Country.

From the 50's Rock 'n Roll, to the me-centric 60's, to the 70's and 80's and on, popular music was brilliant and fun. Melody and harmony and lyrics that were so easy to repeat… Constantly filling the mind and our appetites with their own uniqueness. There was a subtle undercurrent in much that was repetition of a simple phrase… over and over. Simplistic and repetitive. Seductive too. Couldn't get enough of it for my hi-fi.

Any life-meaning direction?? Little… other than a celebration of love embraced…or… love gone astray. Captivating, but mostly shallow.

In the other world… and… from day one… is Country. Blake Shelton Country, George Jones Country, Reba Country… the list is endless. But…THEY ALL TELL STORIES. Rich with content and value. Sure… much

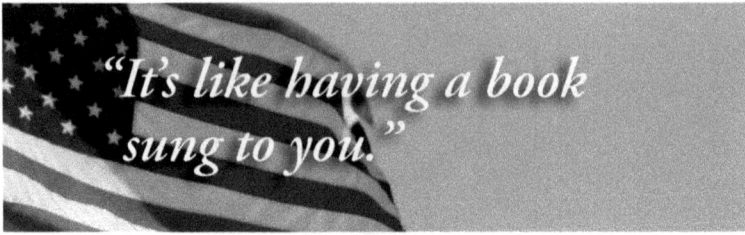

about tragedy, but always therein a message… and advice… Listen carefully to all the soul-felt lyrics of Country music. I will from now on. It's like having a book sung to you.

Of course, you have to get off your sophisticated duff, shed one's judgment robes, and smile again. Sure… there is a good sprinkling of Jesus… wonder what they got wrong?? But try to ignore it and go for the gold. Pure unadulterated entertainment with substance.

I guess you have to live out in the countryside to appreciate it. They call that heartland America. Play on words? Heart Land??

I can move out to the country now just by turning the dial.

See you there.

Gimme another beer.

"Beyond The Pews"

What the heck in the world is a pew? I just checked Wikipedia and it says something to do with long wooden benches in churches with aisles so you can get in and out fast. Then is it "pew" or "phew?" I know many assume the latter. Either way the world tends to avoid both.

You know, nobody wants to be told anything by anybody. Each individual prefers to chart their own course without advice… They don't want advice, they don't need it. And the younger you are the more you complain and "attitude out" when opinion is offered, especially from anyone older.

Ironic, ain't it??? You try to help someone and often your intent is twisted into an offense and walls of feelings arise. "You are hurting me" is the message. Oh well, so what else is new??? We are becoming a culture which is afraid to hurt feelings, so inaction rules. Oh well…

But back to the pews… the non-smelly kind… LOL.

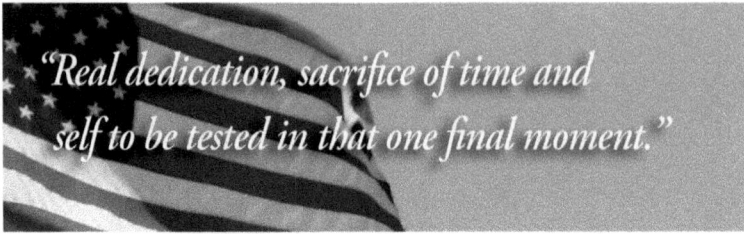

"Real dedication, sacrifice of time and self to be tested in that one final moment."

Pews conjure up the image of sitting in a church with everyone looking at you… and you are supposed to know all about God… I can't imagine anything more unpleasant!!! Waterboarding begins to sound nice… Well, this is how many feel who don't even open a church door, much less the many who are inside… and then sit as far back as possible to avoid judging eyes and take easy exits… Maybe everybody in church should wear sunglasses???

Now, you know what you get in pews??? Pulpit ADVICE… lots of it from the living and the dead. Advice is everywhere. A maelstrom of advice… and they say it is all from God!!! OMG get me out of here… Talk about a marketing nightmare? Make people want to come to church? There is no ad firm willing to take it on. There are so many church haters out there that I keep my opinion to myself… mention church at a cocktail party and you would think you were a serial killer.

They say religion has made a mess of the world. Hey "they"… go back to where you came from. Hidden in religion are values offering the only way out of slavery to self and bigotry. Lost in church histories of shame and hypocrisy are the heroic examples of truth, love, and selflessness. Powerful stories bringing all to their knees in awe. There is enormous good and it is amazing.

A young child senses good and speaks to it, often amazing us. The idealism of youth bespeaks of truth and forgiving good. We still revere character, perseverance, and humility. These stories can be found in the media, but in church they abound in overwhelming poignancy and frequency. Kind of like "seek and ye shall find." The thing is that it requires effort to find out the truth. Spiritual inquisitiveness is not effort free.

We have the courage to climb Mt. Everest without oxygen. But we don't have the courage to enter a church with an open mind.

Take the beautiful Olympics which are testimony to achievement on the purest of scales. No one cheats to the gold, there is no easy way. Real dedication, sacrifice of time and self to be tested in that one final moment. If you win, it was worthwhile. If you lose it can be worthwhile. Discipline and values. Reward lies therein.

If you want to become a Navy SEAL you have to give all you have and more. You are allowed and even encouraged to quit at any moment. Is the achievement worth the pain? To be a good, really good human is the price worth the effort? It means giving up most everything especially the desires of the self. Because to be a really good human you have to care about others more than you care about yourself. This is an insurmountable obstacle for many. Why?

Really good human beings are just regular people who didn't quit...

Don't sell yourself short... Try Church.

God Bless You

"Without A Face"

What would it be like to live without a face? Anyone we don't know has no face. For isn't it the first thing we seem to remember about another person, loved one or one not so loved??? We spend so much time looking at our face. When we brush our teeth first thing in the morning. When we are young we look for blemishes. When older for so many things, but often to privately observe our aging. We don't like to talk about our own faces, but we love to observe others. We put all kinds of stuff on our faces for all kinds of reasons. It seems as if our face is our most important possession. Our faces also contain our eyes through which we observe other faces. And through our eyes we can tell others that we care or that we don't. Amazing thing, faces... What would it be like without them?

Every day we do our best to stay near the faces that please us the most. It is no fun when a face of a person we are not fond of enters the room or our space. Think about work... How the mood so quickly changes with each entering

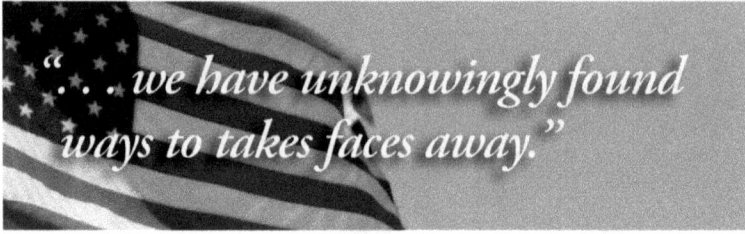
"…we have unknowingly found ways to takes faces away."

face… Think of television, magazines, the newspaper and books… What faces inspire what thoughts and emotions within us? In movies, faces play roles; in fact they are the determining element of the role. We remember the face by the role it played, beautiful or kind or evil or ugly. So many associations for faces… History has all its faces… Angels have faces. We have the face of an angel when we help someone else.

But as our great society has grown we have unknowingly found ways to take faces away. In fact, anything which distances us from one another makes faces fade away. Just walk backwards from someone and see how far apart you can get before their face is no more. Or stand close and cover your eyes, or build a wall of some sort. The more we acquire in wealth or title will put distance between others and us. Who are others, but brothers?

Put me in a prison and I have lost my face to others save the tragic inmate brothers in my cold, walled world. When we build walls around our communities it kind of has a similar

effect. This is happening more and more as we become a society of exclusiveness by all of us who condone exclusion. Just look the other way, it is so easy. Clubs and special groups abound to create security and comfort for members. Clothing and cars and restaurants can also be symbols of exclusion. What is the key denominator of exclusion?…
It is money and its accumulation. Money can be used in powerful ways for good. Yet, those who have money are so much fewer than those who don't. They live with the visible and the invisible symbols of their lack of wealth every day. It hurts… Do they get over it?…

You know, we will help anyone to whom we are close. We will help most anyone whose face we know, well, if we know a little more about them than just their face. We might not like our neighbor, but if he experiences some tragedy or great need we usually rise to the occasion. For his face had more associated with it. In fact, if there is a disaster, we will crawl to our brother, the face next to us and offer assistance. So faces really compel us in so many ways. Yet today, so many are poor and few are rich. But we paint our world as if most are rich and that any form of poverty is a social problem to be remedied by social programs. The most applauded form of assistance is writing checks. It offers an easy protocol and allows us to remain at the preferred distance from our poor. We like the idiom that anyone can become rich if they just work hard. It doesn't work out that way and many just work, work, work, work. Low paying jobs, several jobs, seven days a week 24/7... all this is known to them, but not so much to those who are in that other blessed half of our economy. To the rich, the poor often have no face. Oh yes, they get their tips and their smiles as the patrons patronize them. Yet, they are really faceless. They don't live in the gated communities... They live elsewhere, beyond those walls, but every day they are there serving, repairing, cleaning, digging, ringing up sales, bagging. It becomes endless. We are not necessarily talking about the homeless; we can talk about those just hanging on to their homes or rentals. With dignity and courage they keep on keepin' on.

It follows that we can give them back their faces by learning their names. It is imperative that we address as many people as possible by their names. It is imperative that we genuinely ask about their well-being. For, in time, we will know more about their faces, we will trust our hearts, and hopefully feel comfortable enough to find a way to help. Never has material accumulation been greater. Never has facelessness been greater. Never has the need been greater to create community that transcends economic and cultural walls. Never has the need been greater for each individual to give faces back to others. Put faces on the Hispanics, put faces on the African-Americans, put faces on the Orientals, put faces on the Anglos, yes all the whites, all the races, all the categories of all peoples. But to put a face on someone you have to get closer to them, not further away. Where to start??? Start with the next person you meet. Start in the grocery store. Pick out one clerk and go to her regularly! Learn to say "God Bless You" to every person. What has happened to us? Do we really stop and look hard in the mirror? Do we see a face?

"You Can't Take It With You"

Someone once said to me, "Live it up, you can't take it with you." Over the years I forgot about it until I started to notice unusual generosities and kindness. I had been in a world distanced from pain, where everybody worked hard, dined well, had good homes, and generally enjoyed life. It was only when my life circumstances had me working in a soup kitchen and then a homeless shelter did I get the sense that there was much more pain and need in this world than I had ever imagined. It was all supposed to be in Latin America, India, and all the distant lands... Not in every city and town I had lived in, that's for sure.

I had been a member of the conspicuous consumption club. Socially and materially well off, we spent our means... charged and paid bills and were seldom for real want. I had successfully distanced myself from the poor and made myself relatively irrelevant.

> *" 'There but for the grace of God'*
> *rings in my mind."*

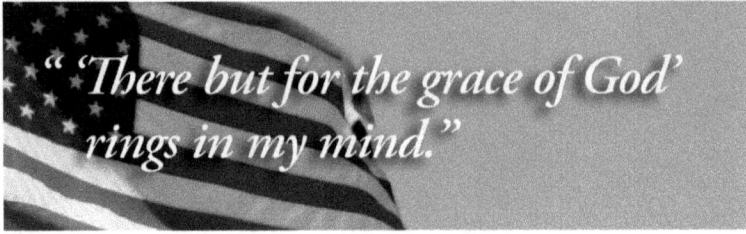

When working fulltime for the homeless shelter in a fundraising capacity, I got to know many of the local non-profits and churches. Contrary to public opinion, they had to scratch for donations. Month to month most survived. Yet the poor they served could not be helped the way we truly wanted... And I began thinking... the way they deserved... but that is a personal judgment... And yet a judgment that we all will someday have to honestly face. When I was distant from the poor, I could not see the pain, much less feel it. My gated community ensured my peace.

As wealth accumulates we work hard on finding ways to spend it and to protect it. If you can't take it with you, then why not the expensive car, vacation, home, wine, etc.??? You can't take it with YOU. For those most fortunate there are trusts to keep the wealth in the family... money that validates the heritage.

But this all seems to be folly. Our first real responsibility is to the living. That is how we can protect the future. Our legacy must be rooted in the present. We must take care of every injustice that crosses our immediate path. We must bring dignity to the moment and equality to the glance. I have come across so many wonderful, valid people whose circumstances are so different than mine. "There but for the grace of God" rings in my mind. If I want to enable and ennoble my kids and friends then I must act in such a way to be remembered. Not by spending on myself, but by giving time and money to the needs of the less fortunate. Not casual, socially acceptable giving but by getting out there in real world where the less fortunate struggle. You can't take it with you has to have something more to it, maybe it should mean giving of myself rather than spending on myself. Contemporary clichés like this buffer us from the truth of our responsibility to one another.

Conspicuous consumption is a virus. There is no Norton Anti-Virus software for this problem. The anti-virus is our heart, not clichés. I must journey back into my heart and conscience to find the spirit of truth and the drive to force myself to look at reality. I get no greater pleasure than from being able to help someone, anyone, directly. Whether it is in a church ministry, volunteering for a non-profit, or other entities that directly serve the poor, I must leave behind money and time where it counts. God help me if my legacy is myself, my possessions, or my travels. My kids will someday understand.

"Manhood"

What makes a man? When we are youths our ears always pick up on phrases about manhood… "That's a real man", "Real men don't cry", or "That man is a hero", etc. We have all heard our own variants… but something hit a chord. We wanted to be a man.

How does that happen? An extreme is "Don't act like a girl", "Men gotta do what men gotta do", which means keeping it inside and keeping a strong front. "Take care of your sister or brother"… "Do what you are told or…"

Soon comes the world of sports and we men are pitted against one another. It is tough until we get into the game and realize we won't actually be killed. It's man against man, though we are boys. Or it is an individual sport where we have to beat every other individual. It requires giving of oneself to a maximum effort. If it is a team sport we learn the hard way that the team, not the individual, achieves the goal. All these are wonderful molding experiences.

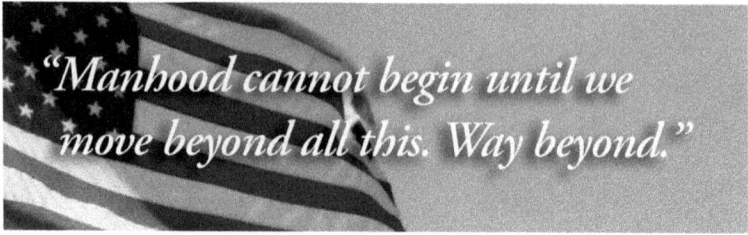

> *"Manhood cannot begin until we move beyond all this. Way beyond."*

Seeming adulthood enters. First jobs. When am I going to get married? Will I ever have a family? When will I be a father? What do I do with so many rules and authority figures in my professional environment? The values of my workplace now intrude into this yet unformed equation. Thank God for beer and sports and any distraction... How much I make quickly becomes the parameter by which I judge myself. Note that this is what I think is important to others. All one's life the opinions of others all too often drove my sense of self... Money, money, money...

This appears to be the solution to all need. Thinking starts to become derivative of this drive. The self becomes subservient to this master??? It is human nature to resist the unnatural. To solely be an entity of money fights against one's inner core and deeply private spirit. We feel it, but often cannot articulate it. We may start to exist on a selfish agenda, though so subtle that we might never be able to admit or see it.

Manhood cannot begin until we move beyond all this. Way beyond. For many it is too late, they are captive to self and dreams of material enhancement which is their equation for success and mastery of life…as they perceive it…

Manhood has reached a crisis point. Status quo, or…??? What is the alternative if not the focus on self???

What is the alternative if not the focus on self??? Stop.

"Grammy Died"

Grammy died. A scream echoed in the deep recesses of daughters and granddaughters. All Grammies die. Why? I ask myself why?

In the spring of life the tiny buds of green appear from nowhere. Little flowers then peek forth like in first dresses. Soon immense blossoming erupts in a sea of color thrown to the skies. All eyes are in awe of the beauty and innocence of this fragile symphony. Then come winds and rain and weathering shows its face. Then fall and winter. But the beauty witnessed is never forgotten. For there was the moment never stolen where beauty was possessed and made eternal in the reflection of the mirror and soul. Beauty defined by the blossom or beauty defined by the soul? Petals limp, color drained, beauty frozen in a kiss. A daughter leaning over the ashen face.

Mortality is seldom respected as the spirit of eternal youth deludes even the most educated. Mortality defines the

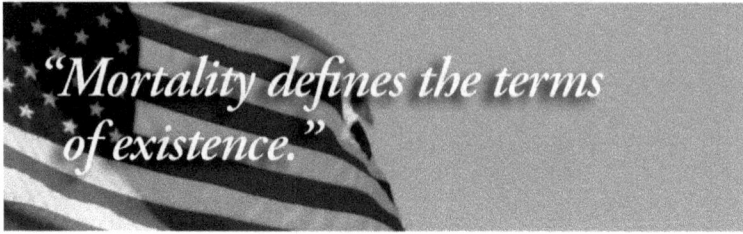

terms of existence. It has taken me a lifetime to become humbled by the awesome miracle of creation. How precious is every child. How precious is every teen. How precious is every mother. How precious is every grandfather.

We are so caught up in the entertainment of life that we overlook the majesty of its delicate hypothesis. And that what is good is more important than evil. Good can prevail only by choice. Choices that every individual makes either consciously or otherwise. As a mother protects her child or as a father protects his business, good and gain endure only by choice.

Today entertainment obscures the value and timing of choice. Even before we brush our teeth in the morning the TV must go on so we can see what might have happened overnight. Once we are caught up with the newest celebrity divorce we feel comfortable to address the mirror and all its demands before grabbing our iPhone to check the last text or e-mail. Hopefully we received something from someone that might allow a response and we are ALIVE. Ready to take on the amazing quantity of texting choices of the day. Starbucks at 8.

Deep down inside every person is a voice. Deep down inside everyone is a prodding to make the good choice. Some call it conscience. Some call it guilt. Some call it stupid. Some call it wisdom wasted. I call it a Spirit of Truth. Most don't care. Whatever. Find out for yourself.

Where do we then build our character based on good choice? I would like to compare myself to others by saying I have made more good choices than you. LOL. Kids look up to those who make the good choices. Not the money choices but the values choices. We want our role models to be the "goodest" possible. Right? Thank God we have media to review the stories of all the role models in all categories so we can feel that humans can achieve that level of good. Thank Good.

Why in the world am I going on all the time about good? Well, because Grammy was really good. Her goodness touched all the kids. Her last years were not good but her family tended to her and that was good. She got hurt by church but not by God. The lips touched the cold forehead.

Goodbye Grammy.

"Birth"

Last chapter first is the title which is the farthest from birth. But that is how life is. Now is where we are and birth was where we started. We started? I started? Birth is a miracle to some. A glorious miracle. Especially if it is your own birth. To many it is an evolutionary event, which still, also defies description. At birth I became me... or at least the beginning of me...

Amazing how girls turn out so pretty. Amazing how so many kids live in surroundings that are so ugly. Amazing at how the year of your birth defines your history. The history of the world at that moment is the beginning from which you make a difference to those around you if... you so choose.

We might not have chosen our birth but what we do with it is up to us. As we grow and as the mirror begins to interest us we have a choice to keep looking at the mirror or to ignore the physical and start to search the unseen. For it

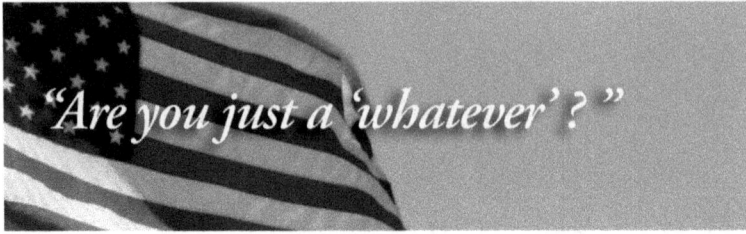
"Are you just a 'whatever'?"

is what we cannot see that is the most important part of forming our last chapter. Do we choose to see what we cannot see to define who we might be? The birth of the unseen? That is our most important choice.

Hope is unseen. Faith is unseen. Your choice. For without either existence borders on the irrelevant. Values seem to be important to the outcomes of life. Some exceedingly bright people contend they are the causes of wars and poverty. To others values forge truth and behavior that affirm hope and faith.

Birth. What is it all about Alfie? What is the meaning of life? If it is meaningless then it is only about endless wars and misery. They keep us busy fighting or avoiding until our life is over and our birth is invalidated. Evolution is a scientific distraction to occupy intellects until they die and become part of the dust of evolution. I just cannot ascribe to these dark and negative notions.

I don't understand life but I sure believe there is more to it. Good is something good. Kindness is something kind. Honesty is something honest. Unselfishness is just unselfish. These are the bricks of something profoundly important. These are the bricks of values. These are the bricks of meaningful human behavior. These are the bricks you want to build your house with.

Is birth meaningless? Are you pro birth or pro death? Are you pro values or pro "who cares?" Is your own birth of any consequence to you or your family? Are you just a "whatever?" Are you a God or a no-God person? Not questions to dismiss unless you are stupid. Really stupid.

Love. You did not know love prior to birth. Is that not a reason just to love birth? Have we not found love to be powerful in our lives? Without it we hide and are insecure. Without it we turn to substitutes that are painful and self-deprecating. Lovelessness really is at the root of all discord and false philosophy… and false religion. Birth must be consummated by love or forget it. Do I want my kid to have values? Do I want my kids to know love?

Darn it, birth creates so many decisions.

I wish birth would go away.

Thank God for December 25th.

"Fashion Week"

I grew up in the world of fashion. It provided a lot of work for many hard working families. Fortunes were made and fortunes were lost. Design can be art. Art that can be worn. The individual can be individual. You can find great art to wear at a TJ Maxx for nothing. Or you can find great art to wear on Fifth Avenue for prices beyond imagination. Women scrutinize women incessantly to figure out what the secrets may be to attract Mr. Right or Mr. Wrong. We let them do it. We let the frenzy be fed. Both sexes participate fully in this dance of appearance.

How do I look? Tell me, mirror. Tell me, friend. Tell me, glance. Do I look good to you?

I dress for work. I dress for play. I dress for sport. I dress for dinner. I dress for the funeral.

I watch television to see who dresses the way I think I might like. We talk about what "celeb" was wearing or how her hair or accessory or makeup looked. A lot to talk about.

"Do I look good to you?"

Does George look better than me? Just kidding... or am I???

Over a lifetime fashions have come and gone and come back again. Look at your old photos. You looked so great at the time and now those looks don't look so cool... obsession with appearance? No... just the ebb and flow of image. Oh, that sounds like an appearance addiction...???

What am I? Maybe it is what I do that enhances my appearance, my image? I work. OK, where, what? How hard??? If I work very hard I may not have extra time for appearance. Maybe. I study everyone to see how they look and how hard they work. You can tell the ones who spend more time on appearances.

Most of our lives we keep redefining ourselves by what we think others think of us. Self image consumes so much energy. Is this who we were meant to be? Do we envy those who achieve self image that is cool? Is there substance to this?

What means more? What means less? Does title, wealth, trips, cars, the way you look mean the most? Why do eulogies so often talk about what one had, not what one gave?

Giving has nothing to do with a checkbook, it has to do with time and effort. "She gave up everything to care for her sick child", "He gave up his position to work with the needy", "She worked hard so others might have their jobs for as long as possible", "He never said no to a hand he could hold", "He drove all night to be there for her." These are stories we have all heard and these are the trappings of what is really cool.

Fashion can be the way you fashion yourself. Fashion can be what you consider to be important. What they say about you. Yes, what we do for others is what real appearance is all about. What we wear or own is irrelevant. The title on the door is meaningless if it is always open.

The burden of self image is not what life is about.

"In Security"

Security is the most wonderful feeling there is. In security must mean in a secure place where nothing can hurt you. You can be in prison and be secure if no one is trying to kill you. In prison there are cameras everywhere making sure things are secure. We now have cameras for business and for public places and for the home to ensure we have a record of our security.

Can you imagine all the recording that is going on worldwide to ensure that we have a picture and video of anything which creates a problem. Wow, glad we have moved beyond tape cassettes. There would be enough tape to go to the moon and back six times. Rest assured the thief or criminal has more to be careful of. Of course anywhere we go we are probably on a tape, or… memory, or some feed. Have you ever seen London and all the cameras? I don't mean to drone on but our drones and satellites are ever vigilant.

"It is a lifelong battle worrying . . ."

Then, why is there still so much crime? Guess there are just not enough cameras yet... I am beginning to get insecure about being secure. Cameras are there to keep us honest. Seeing as how values no longer keep us honest, thank God we have cameras.

What is it with man always getting into trouble? Can some person give me the answer? Have we not learned any one thing from the past???

Whenever a war ends we say "Never again, this is the last war." Then we reduce our military and live happily ever after until... the next war. Then we scramble to build the new weapons of security and of course our economies boom as we come together with a sense of insecurity urgency. Ok, some individual or nation became bad and a threat to something, maybe even values, and it starts all over again... I want my "blankie"... "I want to be secure" is our primal scream.

Insecurity. Boy... do we all suffer from it. Not the physical kind of insecurity but the personal, mental kind. It is really bad in our teens when our self-image is just forming in a culture of emotional chaos.

We are so concerned about how others perceive us that we become dysfunctional. Vanity creates insecurity. Self-indulgence creates insecurity. Self-centeredness creates insecurity. Insensitivity creates insecurity. You can go on and on about the things that embarrass... that diminish self-image and feed insecurity. It is a lifelong battle worrying about what others are thinking of you...

The big purchase is usually a cover for insecurity... everyone has some form of symbolic Yacht which flags insecurity under the guise of innocent pleasure...

When you know who you really are, substantive security begins to shape you. But if your life remains centered in self, peace will be elusive and unattainable. When the light bulb goes on and you find that the center of your being has moved to helping others, often in the least significant of ways, you will find meaning. Standing up for values makes you a warrior of the currently insignificant... Which is significant.

I am not going to tell you what values are, you have to search them out. Some are hidden in those you respect. Some are hidden in our Constitution. But the majority are hidden in the Bible... and a child's eyes.

"They Say"

I am always being corrected by "them"… You know that "they say" the housing market is going to explode. You know "they say" that if Iran gets the bomb, there will be chaos. You know "they say" that it is often bad to be good or vice versa. You know Christopher "they say" you shouldn't talk about what you believe.

I am not "just saying"… I am saying what "they say". So we all had better listen carefully whenever anyone starts a sentence with a "they say". Because an obvious scientific poll has already been taken that convincingly points to the truth that "they say" espouse. We all are so lucky that we have such assurance available.

The fact is that those of us who use "they say" as part of our verbal tool kit are afraid to say what we believe. "They say" is an admission, or, at least signal that we are not personally convinced of what we speak. In other words, it points to our insecurity and ignorance. Fine me $50 every time I use a

"What we say is important."

"they say" to give substance to my argument. Shame on me. Give it to the poor or better yet a fund to re-establish English and grammar in our schools.

What have we become? Where has our backbone gone? Why are we so willing to defer responsibility? "They say" it is because we have become so concerned with criticism that we have sacrificed our identity, our uniqueness, to be safe. What kind of message does this send to our children? I think it says be so careful that you should never step out or take any kind of risk. It is the philosophical breeding ground for mediocrity and failure. Oversensitivity to sensitivity. Hmmm…???

You know (already wrote one on "you know" LOL) we have a lot of soul searching to do. We are facing an important election. By the time you read this it will all be over… but we have important choices to make all the time. Our problem is that we don't know how important they are. It is the little decisions that are often the most significant… yet we tend to look the other way and dismiss the small… Especially if it may involve someone else. The most important decisions are every decision!!! When a young person or some other person sees our decision they reflect on it, consciously or unconsciously. A seed is planted about you and me that defines reality and what values have meaning.

Each of us is a living, important definer of existence. What we say is important and what matters, not what "they say". Whoa… whoa… You kidding me? Hey I am a good father who works, likes football and beer. You are saying "I am a definer of existence???" Whoa… I did not sign on for that. Don't throw that big philosophical stuff at me.

Leave me alone.

"They say" I have my rights.

"Genuine Leather"

I just bought a new wallet. I have a wonderful canvas one from Eagle Creek that is rough and outdoor cool that I have stuck in my back pocket for 10 years. I like it being crusty. My wife doesn't. We were traveling and more concerned about security so I needed to put it in my front pocket. It was too bulky... I kept years of stuff in it. All I really needed was two credit cards and a driver's license... oh, yeah, and my pacemaker card...

So we were in a medieval Italian town with the narrow cobblestone streets and I started looking for the slim leather kind that I had abhorred in the past. And there it was, at the right price. It felt nice. Real leather. And there was this beautifully embossed stamping that said "Genuine Leather". I like it. I like the feel. Now I like the look. I will show it to you.

This made me think about times gone by when "genuine" meant more... It is a new time and science has yielded so

"What is genuine?"

many new materials and ways to make things. Many are truly terrific and what we have always imagined. I love my synthetic, not cotton, canvas luggage with wheels.

But along with amazing increases in product quality there are still artisans out there doing it the old-fashioned way. It is fun to find them and marvel at their skill and dedication. However, over the years we have used the word genuine in non-genuine ways. Saying that this is 'genuine" when it is not. So today we are wary of anything claiming to be genuine. Ha! Isn't that a reversal? We can no longer trust what we trust. Huuhh???

Genuine leather… it still feels so wonderful… it is now a luxury to even have it as a trim…

What is genuine? I hope I am genuine. I know that my journey went through some periods when I was not when I thought I was… I now am.

I do not care what "they say". I am no longer hostage to what others might think of me. If one thinks I am not genuine then "too bad". Not my concern.

If politicians were more genuine they could agree. If politicians cared more about us we could be genuine. If our neighbor cared more about being genuine we could have neighborhoods again.

If we were more genuine with ourselves we could see debt as an enemy, not a privilege. Our kids need to feel that adults are genuine, not self seekers. Our future is our kids and many more of us need to be the best example we can. We need to point out the value of being genuine again. The cancer of single momhood needs to be eradicated. Fathers need to be genuine again and take pride in the acceptance of responsibility. Let's make genuine a path to walk. Let's make genuine the effort we give. A tear is genuine. A drop of blood is genuine. A Cross is genuine.

I am genuine leather.

"Sin Is Just Bad Fun"

Thank God, my name is not on the list. You know, the list of guys in Kennebunk, Maine who were playing Zumba for all kinds of pleasures. Darn it the gal got caught and the police are obligated to put all the names of the pleasure seekers on their Police Blotter. There was this actual debate as to whether it was fair for their names to be made public.

It seems as if we have created a culture and fraternity of who got away with what. Politicians refuse to make hard, honest decisions. Wall Streeters often look the other way than at the bottom line. Bankers just want to bank regardless of proprieties. Moral rightness is too often an obstacle to profit or truth. Think about it… being moral is now politicized to being on the far right… hmmm… beautiful… So what is fair to the guys on the list? You and I both know that sin is just bad fun. Why should you or your family be punished because of the type of fun you were having??? Why??? Looks like Kennebunk has finally put herself on the map. It is important that this is Kennebunk

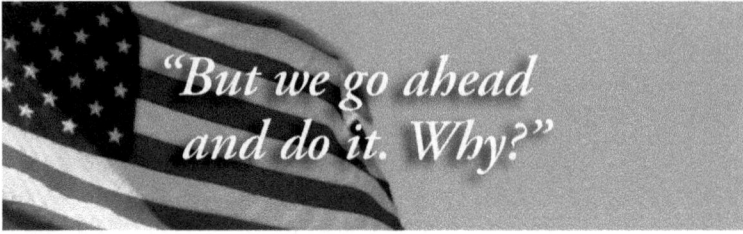

not Kennebunkport... LOL Much ado about nothing other than fun... well... a certain kind of fun... Scarlet Letter kind of fun...

We have a legal system that has refined and defined all kinds of bad activities from murder to lying under oath. False misrepresentation to stealing to abuse to dealing. You get into this world and your name is in the blotter. We know that we will be made public if we do wrong. We know that our family will find out and be hurt. But we go ahead and do it. Why??? Ok... prostitution is only really just bad fun. And it feels so good not to get caught. It is addictive and really fulfilling. If you don't get caught.

Oops all mothers kind of think it is really bad. The government with its laws says it is bad. Are they right? Or is it just bad fun???

Will we step up to the plate and answer this question? We appear to have withdrawn from conflict that involves stating a personal position on most things as we try to sort out all the liberal nuances to every decision. Then we have the mandates of the right??? Oops the right that others now call wrong. We are entering important philosophical arenas where only gladiators of truth and deceit survive. Which are we?

What is truth if it has been so parsed by a legal system that has become a god unto itself. Where is the God of love, compassion, fairness, and truth? Why have we abandoned Him?

After all, sin is just bad fun.

"DDG 112 Hooyah"

When something bad happens we all stop our moment and react. Like when the earthquake was felt this week. My wife and her girlfriends got scared and confused. Natural. But when I talked with my buddies their immediate reaction was as mine... "What do I do right now?" "Who needs to be protected and how?" That is OK, that is the way life has been created. Nurture or protect, our primal roles.

Some things are meant to be natural, left alone... as they are part of nature, our nature. We are born. We die. This is natural. This is accepted. We can leave it alone or we can try to alter. Man can dignify it or man can desecrate it. Good or evil. Selflessness or selfishness.

Peoples' lives can pay tribute to life or they can cheapify it... (New word, cheapify, or cheapen... I like cheapify...) Hitler made life cheap. Our soldiers ennobled it. Love makes life beautiful. Addictions make life ugly.

"What one does for others is the measure of one's life."

When something bad happens something has to be done about it. "Done" does not mean debate! "Done" does not mean politicize. Nike says "Just do it". So do I. Attack bad, don't dither it. Inaction is the very worst form of action.

We have a military because history has taught some of us that bad things have and do happen. Diplomacy works often but not always. There are people who lie no matter how much we give and try to understand. We may even have to act without anyone else's permission. While all the public posturing is going on, there is not a day when someone in the military is not somewhere operating covertly, much less an innocent drone hovering for the next "perfect" kill. Our Special Operations and Intelligence communities have their lives on the line daily to allow us the delicacy of thinking peace is at hand, that we are safe. If something goes bad... our good guys are sent to situations you would cringe at, or withdraw into psychosis.

DDG 112 USS Michael Murphy was commissioned and launched in NYC last week. I was honored to be at the christening in Maine the year prior. I knew Mike at the start of his journey. Many of you may have read the book "Lone Survivor." Mike was a SEAL officer who was sent really deep into the bad. On a lonely mountain in Afghanistan he and two of his men were killed by the Taliban. One miraculously escaped and lives to tell the story. Mike took his final bullets standing with his radio so he could get clear transmission.

What one does for others is the measure of one's life. You can take bullets on a hill or you can take criticism in your home. It does not matter as long as you are standing up for good. Calling a spade a spade... calling bad for what it is, period.

We have become passive in our beliefs. We have become afraid to say out loud what we really feel, what our heart tells us. We don't listen to our heart because it may be politically incorrect. Proactive or passive about life? About values? About evil?

At the end of the commissioning ceremony on the Hudson River a yell by the 1000 people there of "HOOYAH MIKE" resonated in the piers and hearts nearby. When I was told this, my stomach turned and my heart became so heavy... and tears... because the word

"Hooyah" is so unique to a very special community in Naval Special Warfare to which I once belonged.

Godspeed & Hooyah Mike.

"Looks and Beauty"

What looks like beauty is looks. Boy, is she good looking. She is beautiful. As I stared across the room at this hair and face that caught my attention I became mesmerized. I could not take my eyes off her. I wanted her. I had the feeling that we were soul-mates and that life with her would be perfect. She was a 60th Anniversary Corvette.

Hey guys... have you been there? Life is a showroom? You know that your radar is on whenever you enter a restaurant, bar, beach, or bank... or wherever...Capiche?

What is it that catches your attention? Yep, the looks. The looks only... The curves, the fenders. You got to get up close to look inside. Yesss... leather and dials and knobs... And the starter. With a Corvette you know what you are getting, performance and identity. But with a woman you have no clue. The best hair, the best dress, the best eyes... You have no clue. But you don't care as looks are what counts.

"We judge by the cover."

We judge by the cover. We want someone to look the way we want. We want someone we vote for to look good. If they look good then we are comfortable as we want others who like things to look a certain way to like the same looks that we do.

But looks have nothing to do with soul... with what is inside. We learn this the hard way and probably hurt some fine women along the way. It takes a good amount of quality time away from the wine to find comfort and commitment. When looks become secondary we have arrived at the beginning.

My daughter made an award winning film called Shooting Beauty. It is a supersonic emotional flight into what we want to know... the truth of manhood. If you turn away you lose it. If you walk straight forward and take the hand of one who has been dealt a weak one... then you will taste beauty. If you help the afflicted to smile and laugh you will trigger their beauty. Your beauty emerges in the reflection of theirs... When you can bring this to someone in need, not in a bar but on their humble home turf, you will never turn back.

Most of us fear to go where we are really needed. Most have let their values erode so they no longer have the eyes of greatness. They hide behind the laughter of the group rather than standing alone with the denied.

My God, are my daughters beautiful. Inside are temples of compassion and love. Your own child is yours alone to mold. They are the canvas of life and we are the brush. They form their outside, but we paint their inside. "Beauty lies within" we have always been told. Why don't we listen?

Maybe it's our ears? Maybe it's our eyes? How do we get so misled? Deep down in our hearts we kind of know the Truth. But looks got in the way of beauty.

Vroom, vroom. Six-speed with paddle shifters…

"Reverse Racism"

Goes around, comes around…

Slavery. Religion. Wealth. Poverty. Democracy. Socialism. Communism. Materialism. Informationalism.

In our lives we have seen societies stand still, cultures regress, and justice debated…or some would say deleted…

We killed Martin Luther King. Oops… Don't go there… We, meaning a culture that had not been able to find values universal enough to create barriers to evil and prejudice. We have proceeded down a road where everything that was black or white has become a new shade of grey. Laws were established that try to blind one to race rather than embrace it. Subtle, but just as dangerous. Think about it.

Religion has been morphed into an avoidance category. Wealth and poverty are now both evil. Democracy bows her noble knee to lesser. Socialism and Communism are failures for the people. Materialism is celebrated as it strips the soul of worth.

And lastly, the new "Informationalism" is our last hope. With the god of Google we hopefully have all the facts. All the facts, past and present!!! Truth. Truth sought since Biblical times. Truth at last. Thank God almighty Truth at last...

OK, with media and educators alike having equal access to truth how are we doing??? We have spy satellites and information gathering capabilities beyond imagination. We are all in data mines. You could say our identities are slaves to the data mining industry... Interesting twist??? It's ok with me as I no longer have anything to hide anyway...

Are we better off? Are we doing better???

As we ponder the polls and data of politics we see enormous demographic evolutions in America. Ethnic minorities are becoming the new majorities. People of color are getting their own languages legalized. When was the last time you saw a warranty in English only? Race boxes on forms are increasing. You can't say white... it's Caucasian... Who ever heard of Caucasian??? I am finally insecure about saying white. What do I say? And … I am becoming the new minority. Goes around, comes around….

But for sure I am an American, the land of immigrants and opportunity. So is it time to take the race check boxes off all forms??? Reverse discrimination is growing. Now that profiling is such a bad process, what are we left with? What can we base judgments on? Better get a lawyer, the new god of truth. Make sure you have been read your "Informationalism Rights".

As I write this I wonder where it will all lead. In the best country in the world we have raised disagreement to new heights. Our political parties should be ashamed of not being able to raise the dignity of their process. Self-interest pervades decision making.

I like the most recent quote by someone. It is "We the People" not "We the Government". Until we the people re-find our common values based on our Judeo-Christian heritage I fear that this white old man will die with a tear on his cheek.

"Just Saying"

"JUST SAYING"

Is this not a reflection on our culture today where we obsessively avoid criticism while feeling at ease criticizing others???

We choose our media food and I bet we relish the scandals and criticisms of others...

What is the STAR or the ENQUIRER? Bet we all know... JS.

I'm JS that your manhood is also determined by how thoughts are formed and how we choose to have them come out of our mouth.

There used to be elegance to diction and expression.

It is now a hodgepodge of street and ethnic jargon that makes one wonder what speech will be like in the next 100 years.

". . . a hodgepodge of street and ethnic jargon . . ."

Mumbles of sounds and vocabulary that gamers and computer wonks decode effortlessly while the rest of us submit to verbal extinction.

Maybe this happens to every generation.

Sure seems more extreme today.

But I am old and clinging to the past.

I'm JS...

whatever...

I'm JS...

whatever...

"Complexities of Perplexities"

I get perplexed by the complexity of my wife's common sense... Life was so simple before this beautifully complex entity took over. I am a protector and provider. I hunt and kill and bring food back to my family. Kinda traditional. But during this century I have to retreat to my Man Cave. I am perplexed. Do I dare talk to other men? Then in my world there is this phenomenon called "shopping." I never heard it before she put her white dress on. Hmmm??? Do I like to shop??? No... I like to hunt... and not for a handbag.

I don't know why when I make a decision ten other takes on it are offered by my lifemate. Ok, but I want to do it my way. Nope. There will be a manhood-reducing compromise hidden in the lengthy explanation as to why my common sense is not common. Well, now that I have succumbed to the pavlovian training I can begin to see a new logic. It is called listening and agreeing. I'll bet there are 100 million beers being raised as I am welcomed into the club.

But she really is brilliant. I would never see or remember all that she does. And the memory… I don't know why the military and CIA don't have 100,000 wives in this center to provide coherence to intelligence. Just a thought. Maybe one of our politicians could earmark a new deduction for same so it costs nothing other than a new burden of separation on us good guys. I am perplexed.

I sure pray this honesty is not opening up a Pandora's Box.

Ok, now we get down to business. I don't have to physically give birth and mother (manage) every breath of this gift from somewhere. (Don't you love evolution?) I don't have to worry about getting pregnant. I don't have to shop for baby clothes. I don't have to feed my baby from my body. I don't have to lay awake always alert to any different sound. Nope, I get to put a pillow over my head and go to sleep. I get to get away from all this stuff and go to work where there is clear structure and fully organized complexity. I am a provider. I am a good guy. I am perplexed.

My wife had better keep her looks up though. That is what brought me to her, lucky thing. I do not want her to be a single parent. I'll go shopping with her. I am getting to know so many Home Goods and TJ Maxx parking lots. Great place to read and text. Kind of a Mobile Man Cave. Wonder what my buddies are doing? So many are active sports followers. There are so many options for away time… fishing, climbing, motocross, golf, tennis, shooting, kayaking, diving, sailing, surfing… and on and on… men away and really happy. Anxious to return and share their adventure with the wife and children.

So I finish by confessing that I am totally perplexed and totally in awe of the complexity of women. How in the world do any raise kids and work at the same time? A guy worries about his child, but a woman lives that child… And that woman lives that husband. It is so complex that I do lip service to understanding.

I am perplexed. God Bless Them.

"Happy"

My wife said to write something happy and then she would read it. But I am a happy guy. I am happy when I write because I am trying to give something to a reader. Ok, for her, I will try to just make this happy.

Playing with grammar and words makes me happy these days. When I get an e-mail from just one person saying they like something I wrote I am really happy. If my editor at the Naples Daily News prints one of these I am honored happy. I am happy when my kids are happy. I am happy when I know my Navy buddies are ok. These days for any of us it is good when anyone we know is ok. Ok is the new happy. It is no longer as easy to be happy. I don't mean beer or wine happy. I mean inside happy.

We have dogs. I dare not tell you the truth how many. But their eyes are deep pools of trust. All animals have no choice but to trust. They just want to be happy. We make sure they are and they make sure we are. That is mega

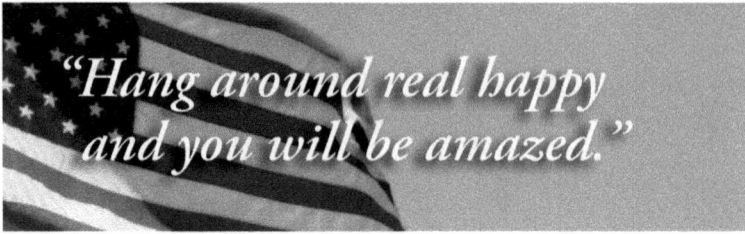

happy. Just to walk around and always be bumping into happy. Need a fix? Got a down moment? Look into any one of those eyes and be seared by their innocence and trust. You gotta feel happy as they put 100% of their existence in your hands. Wow… what an honor! Makes me happy.

Lucy is the oldest. A real old golden. Jowls and brows are now white. Her step is slower and more guarded. Kinda like mine. Then she just looks up wagging her tail like you are giving her her very first bone. Mesmerizing happy. Takes your breath away. Wish I could be more like that. I am sure my wife would concur. LOL.

I am fighting making this heavy and seemingly important…

I know we all spend our whole lives trying to find happy. Hang around real happy and bingo. Not people with false or superficial worldly happy. Make two columns for happy, true and false. Dump all those in the false column. Hurt feelings??? Too bad. Hang around real happy and you will be amazed. Television poses a true test. I know that we guys cannot give up action etc. I know you gals cannot give up celebrity gossip. My wife says she will only watch comedy in this dark world. That makes her happy. Well, duuhh? When she is happy I'll be darned if I ain't happy. 'Course pulling the trigger on a few unhappies would make me happy too. (joke) Let's laugh at what I am writing and be happy.

Really happy people are out of themselves. Really happy people are just helping others. The greatest form of happy is service. When I am serving and taking care of anyone else I am the most happy. My wife works her butt off serving all those who work for us and all those who shop in our stores. You can find her alone in hotels half the year; you can find her at our cash registers at 8:00 in the evening. She of course will disagree, but I see in her more happy than I see in most others. She is too busy to not be happy. I am happy to be there for her. I am happy to be there for my daughters. I am happy to be there for our dogs. I am happy to be there for you.

Have a Happy!

"Why"

How many times can a kid say "Why?" One why leads to another… ad nauseam. Why? This writ is going to drive both of us nuts. Why? Because the word why is going to attack us and we get enough of it all day long as it is.

It all started with our very first "Why Mommy". We didn't understand why we were being asked to do something!!! And when we saw Mom and Dad leaning over and explaining something we didn't really understand we doubled down on our why's?… and there you are.

Wonder when the first why in history was asked. Was Moses the first?… or even Adam when he was given the apple??? Something to think about. Who was the first atheist who asked why? Just kidding. Didn't mean to offend any special interest group. LOL.

This brings me to the problems of today. Now this is crazy… but I fear we are not asking enough "Whys". We have stopped asking as to not bother others or maybe just

"Why don't we have the answers."

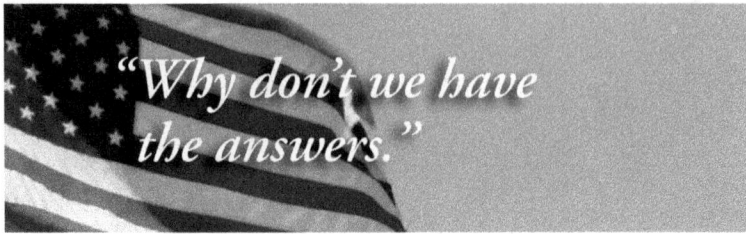

not to bother. To ask a why there has to be a question and an answer sought. But to ask a question may reveal a lack of knowledge. Maybe the person you ask will know and think you are stupid. Now that is painful.

We didn't used to worry so much about what other people thought. Life was simpler and things were more black and white. (Now don't ask me why.) Something has happened to make us more passive or non-committal. We are less confident. Our innocence was not replaced with structure but with doubt as there are so many explanations to everything. And so many people with so many different feelings. And… concurrently… we are insanely more feelings-driven as we don't know what else to trust anymore.

Why does so much of the world not like the USA? Why is there so much hate in the Middle East? Why do we act like there is no real evil or danger? Why does money not solve more problems? No matter where in the world we place it. I think we are not asking the right questions as we are afraid to do so.

Birth and death are wonderful miracles that define all our whys. It's what we do in between that matters and we are losing grip. Can we talk about what is really valuable? Can we talk about what really makes a difference? Can we talk about what is the right way to live? Can we talk about how to best teach and protect our children? Can we talk about what we are not teaching them? Can we ask the young veteran what he has learned overseas? Can we ask him what he believes in?

If we can't ask all these questions… If we can't have these discussions… then who were we really meant to be? Why don't we have the answers? Why don't we want to believe? Why?

"You Won't Believe It"

You won't believe it!! What won't I believe? As you hang me in anticipation until you, yes you, are ready to terminate the suspense. Well it better be good if I have allowed you to toy with my attention...

It seems as if so much more of our time is taken up by the suspense of what is coming next. Teasers infect all advertising, entertainment, and texts. We hang in waiting for answers as they are separated into their "You won't believe it" segments.

"Will it rain tomorrow? Find out after the break!!!" "This break is brought to you by Burma Shave"... Do any of you remember those wonderful suspenseful road signs spaced a hundred yards apart that kept you waiting for the answer...? "No matter / How you slice it / It's still your face / Be humane / Use / Burma-Shave."

Life was good.

You can't believe until you do. What does it take these days to make one a believer? What will it take to get us to not only believe something is wrong but to do something about it? How many innocents must die? How much injustice must be excused?

It almost seems that nothing is right anymore as everything has some group that is unhappy or offended by something that just used to be normal. Would you believe it? Where has the positive gone? What happened to plain old happy?

Like the old Chinese saying, "I work, I happy." That's why I like Chinese restaurants. The fortune cookies keep it simple... and encouraging.

Can I take another one, Mom?

"Pain"

Pain is so confusing. There are so many kinds of pain. Where do you start? Many of us know so little of the pain shouldered by so many. The pain of illness. The pain of injury. The pain of emotional scars. The pain of abuse. The pain of rejection. The pain of insecurity. The pain of prejudice. The pain of snobbery. The pain of indifference. The pain of neglect. The pain of aloneness. The pain of crime. The pain of guilt. The pain of homelessness. The pain of sin. I bet you could add several more???

Each of the above pains is carried inside the individual who often feels a guilt or embarrassment and endures in deep private. It's the inside that hurts the most. Think of how you feel when criticized or accused. It hurts. You look away. You try to find the positive distraction. Sadly, for too many their chosen recourse is alcohol or drugs… or excessive spending… or excessive denial… All take their toll and often bring one to the brink of nihilism, a personal sense of nothingness, of a lost self-worth.

I am writing this as it is triggered by a man named
Dominic. But he is just an insignificant parable to the
millions of suffering. He knows pain from cancers,
surgeries, back, nerves, hands, eye, and things we don't
discuss. His pain has been for years and continues. Then
there is my friend Juan who had a back injury 10 years ago
and has remained in severe pain in spite of an imbedded
morphine pump. These two bear their plight with courage.
This kind of strength is not of this world to which they
both attest. They have chosen not to withdraw into
themselves but to embrace a greater hope. Now I don't talk
about religion so we will leave them alone and choose our
own paths...

These physical abuses to their systems are different
than abuses to the soul which are perpetrated by sin on
another. Disrespect for the individual can have monstrous
ramifications. Sins of sex are the most overlooked and the
most devastating. To rebuild the disrespected innocence
of innocence lost is formidable. It requires forgiveness
and new sources of love. Apologies are nice but not always

forthwith. Forgiveness alone requires great manhood and courage so the perpetrator no longer owns the guilt that devastates the victim. The victim must let go. The victim must be held tight and then cough up the metaphoric blood and purge the hurt. Forgiveness is the only path to freedom.

Lastly, every one of us is infinitely unique. Our scars make us uniquely suited to help some other victim of pain. When we can talk their language as we have felt their pain we can be the angel that holds the key to their prison door. Do not be afraid to hold the hand of one whose vibes you sense. You may be the only saint to exist for that person. Don't sell yourself short. Just do it. Act. Grab that hand. Smile.

Our world is short on saints because we have chosen to become a passive and insecure culture. We are more concerned about sensitivities than the sensible.

Men need to act not dither. Pray for us.

"Shame on Them"

Shame. Never think about it much. Yep, I have some things to be ashamed about. Happened a while ago. Guess most... or many of us can say the same. We kinda keep it to ourselves and move on while trying to make up for it. Life is really about making the best of every new situation that is offered one. Get real. This is the truth. Carry guilt and it will bury you. Get forgiven and you can build upon your wrong. You can mean something in special ways to people you never knew before.

Shame. Hmmm... It is really an ugly word. We love to hear about others' shame. Even that could be considered shameful. When others look the other way as the shamed pass by there is pain. Feel it. It is not nice.

We all have different standards for shame. Usually we are all too ready to judge. And usually the shamed deserve to be judged until... they repent... and ask for forgiveness... Or something like that.

"Usually we are all too ready to judge."

"It's a shame." "Shame on them." "That was shameful…" they whisper. I do not want to do anything that could bring shame on anyone, much less myself. "It's a shame that baby died…" "It's a shame that he did that to her…" It's a shame that our borders leak." "It's a shame that the poor are poor and the rich are rich." "Shame on those laws." "Shame on that disrespect." Gets kinda fun thinking about how many ways one can say, "Shame on them."

I wish I didn't have to take this from the abstract to the specific now. It was a sort of setup. There has been so much tragedy, especially the hurricane. You see… as Americans we rush to the crisis. Guys are coming from all across the USA to serve their grief stricken brothers and help rebuild the shattered homes and lives. Just like 9/11. It is who we are. It is all about our Judeo-Christian heritage and values. Period.

Sadly, this is also about my family, a small and special group of guys who would give their life for you in a heartbeat. We were put through a physical and mental training that reduced you to breathing and believing. SEALs. My time with this community was short compared to these days, but I know who we are. From the Medal of Honor recipients, Mike Monsoor, Mike Murphy, and all the others to the guys currently downrange. Google their stories, go ahead, I dare you. There is not one of us who would not have been on the roof in Benghazi.

It's a shame that nobody came to their rescue. They didn't ask for much. They seldom ever ask… Those two Navy SEALs… But they asked… and we could have been there… even if late… Shame on us for not hearing what we should have heard. Who says you don't fight because you may get hit? It's a shame we lost two of our very best. The response… Fire an Admiral??? Amazing… Medals are due all.

Where is the truth?

Shame on whom?

"The Greatest Democrat"

The greatest Democrat has yet to be born or yet to claim the throne. It is within reach. The greatest Democrat must simplify codes and vision. Values must be reclaimed in clarity. The deserving poor must be embraced, not dehumanized by bureaucracy. Those who work hard must be lauded; those who do not must accept responsibility not handout.

Fairness comes from ethics and morals. A great Democrat cannot parse values. He must stand for truth, compassion, and accountability. Lastly, and most difficult, is to bring all together under a common vision of unity not division. Class and demographic distinction, aka warfare, must be targeted as corrosive and deadly. I could go on, but you get the picture.

In fact, you should take up the lead. In fact, the greatest Democrat should be the greatest Republican, or vice versa.

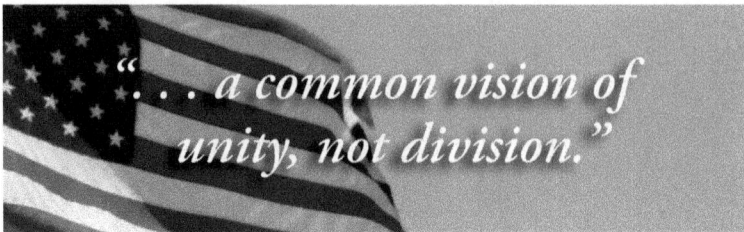

> "...*a common vision of unity, not division.*"

In fact, neither will survive if they don't take off their red and blue ball caps and act like an all-star team against the perils ahead.

"The Tug"

Nope, this is not a story about the tugboat that pulled and pulled the disabled ship back into port. That could be a great analogy.

There is the tug... On your shirtsleeve for attention. You turn to see who it is. If at home you probably know. But if out in the other world, you have no clue. You instantly try to guess. Friend??? Danger??? You don't know until you see the face of the tugger. Male? Female? Child? Authority...??? Your mind runs wild in that micro-second. But isn't that the case with anything you don't know???

Suppose you were the tugger coming up from behind anticipating the tuggee's response...? Fun to catch someone unawares... Well... as long as it is good news... Hmmmm...

Hi Bill, remember me, it's Frank!!! And so on... Unless it is "Mr. Wilson, may I have a word with you?" Turning... "Yes Officer." The tug. The tug may have any level of

"I have my Tug Rights."

significance. It depends on the kind of life one is leading...
Hmmmm...?

Then there is the most important tug of them all. Can you
guess it?... The tug of the heart. Why is this so special?
Your heart is generally, for most, where the truth lies.
"Follow your heart." Heard that before. If all else fails trust
your heart. Why is that??? Is it philosophical? Or is it real?

If something tugs at your heart it may be something you
want. Like a car you just saw. Like the handbag she wants
to buy. Or even as mundane as the candy your child must
have. All kinds of tugs all day long. The material ones fill
giant lists. Christmas is when lots of tugs are fulfilled.

We are creatures of emotions and the tug of an attractive
person conjures up peace and comfort. Wow, so powerful
that we are rendered as children, making questionable
decisions just to yield to this tug. Get out of the way
society... tugs of attraction are covered by the First
Amendment, Freedom of Tugs. We all know about this one.
In fact it is in the courts every day being interpreted and

challenged. I have my Tug Rights. ACTU, American Civil Tugs Union. LOL. Give Me My Tugs or Give Me Death! Forget which state that is...

As you can surmise, I always save the best for last. The very best and most important tug for last. The tug of Truth. When we were kids, something up inside us always tugged at us. It was the tug of right and wrong. Where does it come from? Were we born with it??? But it sure is there. Remember saying for the first time that you said "That was not fair..." Whether it was an act of some other kid or the decision of an adult, you had a clear tug as to the Truth and fairness. As we got older, we became more excusing and able to explain black and white away. To color badly so it was easier to excuse. To smother the innocent tug of Truth so it was muted. Now Truth has a harder time of it becoming a tug as there are so many rules and bureaucracies to ensure tugs do not get out of hand.

But the truth is that the Truth does not have to die in your heart. Feed it the right values and surround it with like Tug seekers and re-champion the Tug of being honest with one's self. Tug yourself off the path of mediocrity and lead or tug others to do the same.

You are only as valuable as your values. Tug on.

"Rules"

Rules are meant to create order and keep one from harm. Rules try to put us on a path that ends in good… Well, it so happens that we did not like the original rules. Guess what? We then wrote more rules to make the original rules easier to manage. OK… Our legal system seemed fine and things hummed along…

Then what the heck happened? This country was founded on principles which came to be out of date??? Go figure! Were our founding fathers just not sensitive enough? Of course, they could have no vision as to the impact of new technologies. Do we still hold their principles to be transcendent and based on the sanctity and worth of the individual? Lofty goals? (Pun intended.)

Now I remain positive about our potential to strive for higher goals. (Last pun intended.) But do we not get it? That more rules and regulations inevitably complicate this journey? Legislators have become the minions of

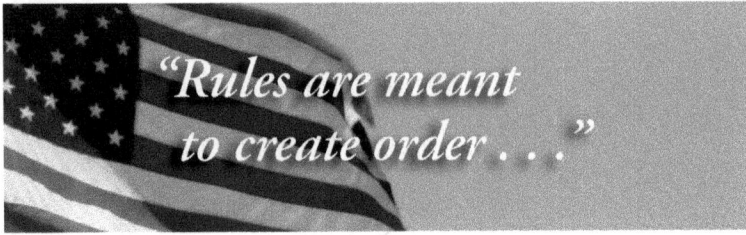

legal technicality. Lawyers are so prolific that they are like waiters in a legal soup kitchen. Lawyers have these ear trumpets affixed to the sound of anyone in disagreement, waiting to issue volumes of self-justification.

Then again, lawyers are our paperwork police. Heroes in a complex world where their long hours looking for truth is a service to all. As long as they are serving us. As long as their principles are lofty and unselfish....

"In order to proceed, click 'agree'," which we do as the associated fine print would require us to have a lawyer. How absurd that they cover their fannies while we can't afford to... CYA is now a driving legal force in every enterprise. Ever try to read the fine print? It is a waste of time. Did you try to read the ballot on Election Day? It was an insult to the voter. Disrespectful in its incoherency.

Rules are now so confusing that they are creating disorder and harm. This is not where we began.

"Labels"

Campbell's Soup. That was the number one label when I was growing up. Red, white, & gold, I think... But one thing not in doubt was what was inside. Campbell's Chicken Noodle Soup. It was the same every time I had it. Must have been a 100 times when I was a kid... That stuff was really good... well, to a ten year old... And come to think when I was in the Navy I had some... and it was full of good memories. A good label... little salty for these days... But when it is cold and you are hungry and you are not in Italy...

It is so nice to know what something is before you commit. Wonder Bread... Boy, was that always good for peanut butter and jelly. Gonna miss it. Bet you all have many labels you know and trust... Hershey's? Today I like Haagen-Dazs...

Nowadays most labels have changed to become more updated and more relevant. They now contain so much

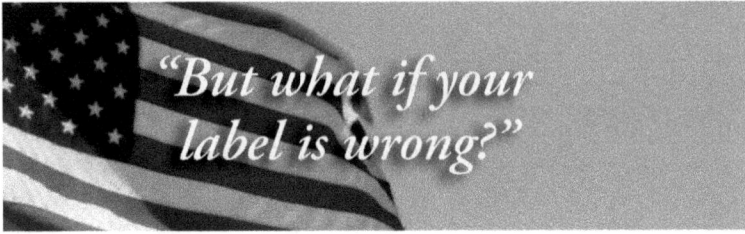

"But what if your label is wrong?"

information and warnings that it has taken some of the simple fun and trust away. Can you really trust a label that has to promise so many things? Labels have become like TV commercials, trying to please your senses while enticing you to buy it or like it or trust it. Insurance companies, banks, etc. promise exactly what you are looking for when you call one of their "Relationship Associates"!!! Makes me want to choke. Promise experts. Then they hand you off to another person just out of training who is now a promise specialist... LOL.

Don't get me started on "voice prompts". Would you believe they even have robots making phone calls that pause when you talk, then continue as if alive???

Labels, they ain't what they used to be. We didn't used to label people so much. As long as I can label them am I in control? Labels put people in judgment categories. Then it is easy to talk about them to others. Kinda safe.

But people really are as simple as they used to be... humans have been smart, good, bad for centuries if not millenniums. Read what they wrote way back then. You could judge people by their values which were more black and white than they are today. Today people are so many shades of grey that you need a lot of labels. But what if your label is wrong??? What if you didn't have the time to get to know the shoes that person walked in? Prejudging is a big politically incorrect sin these days. Yet, no one has the time to evaluate. We have to legislate values. Leave it up to the lawyers…

We have taken the values out of our value system. Old labels and old values are too old. The new ones are more sensitive and discerning, reserving punishment until it is meaningless. You can no longer "just do it" because you might be wrong. Might??? Give me a break. I have my labels backed up by old fashioned values and the label I put on you is going to be as right as Campbell's Soup. Deal with it. In fact, how about I take my Brother Label Maker and print out your label! Label me all you want. I am a Campbell's Soup can.

"The Trident"

The Trident is a symbol for three things. No I am not talking about the Trinity, not today. Do good things come in threes? Wonder what else comes in threes???

How do we survive without threes? How do we just survive? How do we make something out of nothing? Does a child come from nothing? What keeps us from becoming nothing? What happens when we sit around and do nothing? Nothing. Nothing at all. Maybe I should have entitled this piece "Nothing."

If I want to get a driver's license and don't study, what happens??? Nothing. If I don't go to school, what happens??? Nothing. If I don't put any effort into my life what happens? Nothing again. One's life becomes defined by self-inflicted nothingness.

The opposite extreme of this is the pursuit of a thing called the Navy SEAL Trident. Being mega-proficient in three elements... Sea, Air, Land. Exhausting, brutal, cold,

"Do good things come in threes?"

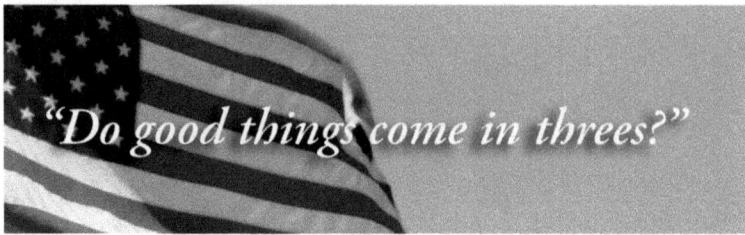

preposterous conditions for months on end. Sleep deprived… running endlessly in sand, swimming endlessly in the cold ocean, and ultimately dropping in the night sky with your wits intact. In and out of any element at any time. Mastery of weapon, mind, and body with perseverance that reduces 90% of those who try to give up. Kind of like life where so many give up on their dreams or values or self.

There is not a day that goes by that you do not read about a tragedy where someone quit. To quit means that to try no longer has value. But if you don't try to do something how do you learn or grow? When they put my first bike in front of me it was scary. Had I not said "no" to fear I never would have known the wonder of a 10-speed or a motorcycle. Had I said no, I would have had no idea of what I was going to miss. No knowledge is the devil of accomplishment.

Today it is as hard finding employees as it is finding employment. Conundrum. Stupid. Hard work brings dignity and sense of self-worth. Blame the worker who underperforms. Blame the company who over-structures and loses the human touch. Profit without ethics is unseen terrorism. Administrative shields have dehumanized communication. We are reaching the sophisticated day when a call to Human Resources is answered by voice prompts… Just wait….

The old fashioned notion of teamwork has been destroyed. Oh, yes, there are teams in corporations with assignments… but for the most part they are jokes.

When I talk Team I know what I am talking about. In fact, look at the world of sports. Team sports. It is amazing what the champions achieve against all odds with an improbable mix of characters. Something intangible happens and they play like a pure team, being able to communicate without words. Analogue, not digital. Capiche?

Same can be said for many small businesses as their team is so tight that they don't need the overhead of excessive administrative activities. Yet with the computerization of all aspects of business today there is no longer a useful team environment where humans feel bonded in task execution. And… the terrain becomes really fertile to quitting and moving on… and quitting and moving on…

This exploration of a quitting-minded culture could be characterized as a moment in history where a society undercut its glory and failed. A time where efficiencies of human interaction were dismissed to a balance sheet. A time where we quit on human.

On a SEAL Team no one has quit who is there. No one will quit regardless of the danger assigned. Being human has returned to basic values and they are worth dying for... the old values that were the foundation of our freedom and our pleasure.

Quit on God and you have nothing...

"Excellence"

Pats on the back. Oh how wonderful they are… and becoming almost extinct were it not for texting… LOL.

Think about how deep inside one secretly yearns for someone to say "Excellent" to something you have done. No… I know… not you… Hahaha… yess… you. You gotta eat food to grow… and you have to have praise to feel alive. Remember when you were young and you heard others getting praise? Or how proud you were if it ever came your way from classmates or parents. Old people like me still remember their youth and praise they may have received… Or when your dad said you were a "good son." Pow… Bam… Yesss… I'll take it any day. Gimme praise and I will give you the world… And a promise never to forget you.

But in all due modesty I won't tell you any more… unless you want to praise my humility… LOL.

On a grander scale… nations, cultures, leaders, and populations of individuals all hunger for praise. Their

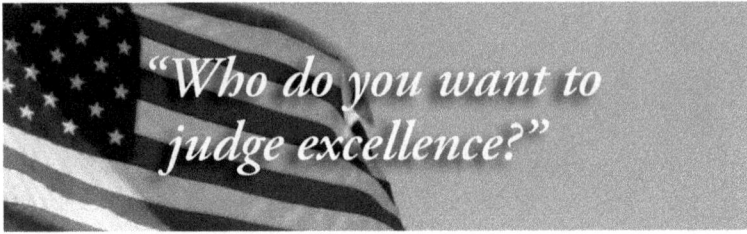

sensitivity and need for praise is shown in their indignation and offense taken when not praised, much less criticized. Even terrorists seek praise. Crazy.

Now there are a million skills that one can excel in with the recognition of "Excellent". From Pulitzer Prize to Academy Awards, they all promote excellence... Well sort of...? It really depends on the interests of the voting mechanisms... Celebrities like to pat celebrities on the back, you know...

Excellence in life? What is that? Huuuhh??? Who awards that??? What medal???

Real, powerful, meaningful excellence is unseen. It is invisible to all but the few. On the battlefield in a flash of brightness and pain? In the hospital room where hands are holding? In a dark alley where "No!" is said to evil? In the home where a father accepts his responsibility and bends over to tuck his daughter in? At that moment where he kneels and says the Lord's Prayer with her?

Who judges excellence?

Who do you want to judge excellence?

Seek it out and award it on your own.

"Precious"

"My precious." I don't think a guy really likes to be called that, certainly not in front of other guys... But I know a gal loves to be called that... and you had better mean it. If you are a gangster, then it really doesn't matter.

Precious jewels come in all kinds of types: rubies, emeralds, diamonds, etc. Now these are really expensive and that is why they are precious stones. We put them in gold settings to show off how precious they are as they glitter and glisten their worth. Sad that they are so precious that you have to be careful when and where you wear them. Don't want the poor to see them...

Children are the most precious. Why??? Because their innocence is so precious. Innocence is a purity that must be carefully submitted to the world while it is cherished and protected. All kinds of life-long scars can be the result of irresponsible innocence management. Yet scars can be the grist of greatness. Succumb to the scar and you have quit

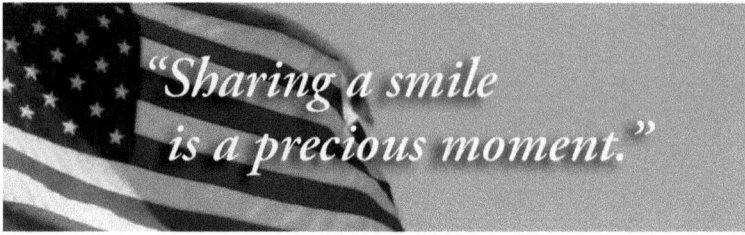

on your potential. The greatest stories come from the survivors of pain, the conquerors of disadvantage. Children lose their innocence one way or another. Protect them as long as possible. It is our precious DNA duty.

There are traits in individuals that are precious. They are as precious as they are inspiring to observe and share. Be it a kindness or a clarity of purpose that serves not the self. There are precious moments with another. Sharing a smile is a precious moment. Bringing dignity to an encounter is precious. Shielding someone from harm is a precious honor. Isn't it wonderful to explore what is precious to us? Think about it.

Love is so precious. Not to have love is life without breath. We so often succumb to contemporary notions of affection and desire. But real love is not about the self. Real love is about protecting the precious, regardless of cost. Real love is protecting, caring, and nurturing one in need, be it spouse, family, neighbor, friend, or the less fortunate. Love is blind.

Eyesight is precious. It is easy to see and be blind. The heart has eyes. It can see Truth. Truth is precious. It is our choice to define what is precious. Our choice. Choice is precious, as is freedom to choose. A precious part of our nation.

Ask a veteran.

Are values precious?

Is good precious?

"Absolutely"

"And that was an interesting traffic jam. Handing off to you Stella!..."

"Absolutely, Carlos. The accident stopped traffic for a while. I'm absolutely sure of that." (NBC News 4)

One has to listen more closely to the media these days as they are the harbingers of vocabulary and grammar. In fact, with the school systems under such criticism, teachers have to tippy toe around every word they say in case it falls into a legal happening. Absolutely. Television is the new reality classroom. Children and adults alike are pounded away with the expressions of violence, domestic discord, irreverent humor and marginalized history. How can a teacher who cares compete??? To add salt to the wound along comes the cell phone and its universal abuse of grammar and focus. Absolutely, heads are all down in the streets of New York as urgent feelings are shared walking to work.

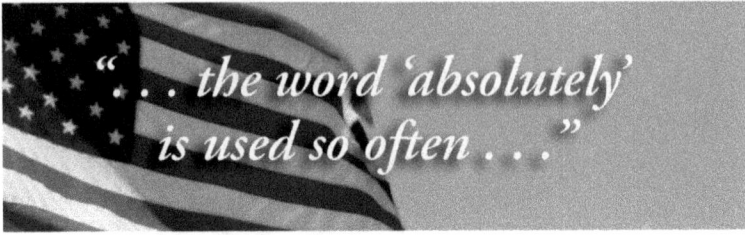
" *. . . the word 'absolutely'*
is used so often . . . "

Oops, back to "absolutely". I like to call it AA. Absolutely
Abuse, as alluded to the word "absolutely" is used so often
and so casually that it ceases to bear any resemblance
to its original worth. It is supposed to give one absolute
assurance that what is being talked about is true and the
speaker can be trusted, absolutely.

But its overuse, like so many other words, has made it
impotent and without meaning.In striving to hide our
insecurity we use words, phrases, and labels to project
conviction. When I hear them I am suspicious and not
trusting. This new cultural wariness actually distances one
from another. Cliché vocabulary is a signal that the person
does not know who he or she is, absolutely...

Text or Twitter or Facebook ...the die is cast.

Woe to be a teacher in a good school, the odds are
absolutely against you.

"Now class, put your cell phones on mute and under your seats and pay attention."

"Today's lesson is how to get a student loan without trying."

"Charity"

"To be or not to be?" is a question all charities have to ask themselves. Their vision is pure. The execution is treacherous. One cannot give now without boundaries and rules and scrutiny and judgments and liabilities. Wow! What if you just want to give?

If your charity starts from genuine Christian compassion you are history. Adios purity, hola political correctness. Want to pray with your clients? Forget it. Want to have Christian symbols on your walls? Forget it… and forget any available government assistance.

Why is a religious affiliation such a problem for us these days? Why do other non-profits have to pretend to be non-Christian to receive government assistance? This is upside down nonsense. No prayer in schools? How stupid. What are we afraid of that our forefathers weren't?

Bigotry cloaked in "correctness." Christianity has endured 2,000 years of self-inflicted wounds and glory. Why is it the

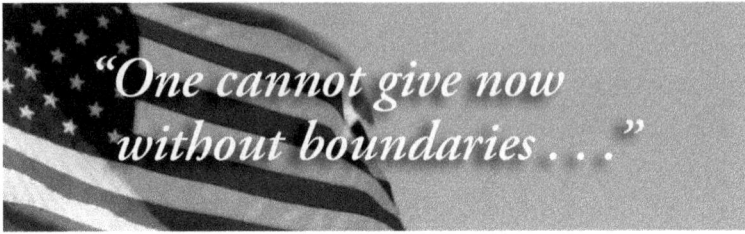

bad guy? We espouse tolerance on so many fronts. We are liberated with our freedoms to protect every sensitivity and every cause. Women's rights, children's rights, bills of rights. I bet you could have "One-Eyed Parrot's Rights"... open up a charity and get federal funding... But if the parrot is a Christian??? Forget it.

Christians these days are intimidated and silent with all the noise going on in the media... much less the stirrings and proclamations in the Middle East. Is it best to be an atheist? Or certainly never share your spiritual leanings out loud in the daytime? I bet a proclaimed atheist will find his own discomfort in Tehran if he doesn't kneel to theirs...

Terrorism is proclaiming believe what we do or die. Your children and families are insignificant to the suicide bomber. OK America, quibble with the funding protocols of charity. Dither in absurdity when your energies should be in strengthening national values and resolve. Unity in compassionate vision with fierce resolve to deny injustice must be carved out of the political quagmire. Leadership requires clear values, not ones that need to be interpreted in 2,000 pages of legalese. Where did we lose our common sense? Things don't get done unless you do it. That is why I love Nike. "Just do it." That is why the Navy SEALs are so good. Think about it.

What is wrong with "The Pledge of Allegiance"?

Let's be proud of our Christianity again. There is simply nothing wrong with it. Jesus was not a bad guy. Millions can attest that they would not have survived without Him.

Can't we all get along before it is too late?

"Eulogy"

When it comes time for the eulogy… who is going to say what?… I wonder if that person is going to say the right thing??? I hope they don't ask that other person to say something. Will my wife be crying? Will my daughters say the right thing?

Sure glad I will be busy elsewhere. Spare me the video.

I hope it will be in a real church with real pews, not on the beach and ocean which I loved a lot too… After my stents and bypass surgery I got to live well beyond my Dad's years if this is an accomplishment. Did the world benefit??? Or at least my world??? Or was I just a consumer? Of time…?

I have heard others' eulogies and they left me kind of cold (pun intended). They talked about the love of family, vacations enjoyed, hobbies and sports. Business career and other accomplishments… even generosities… and "he loved this and that" ad nauseam. For the most part they sound a lot alike.

"Life just can't be about the last years of golf...."

The pursuit of titles, money, or recognition traps so many on a street to nowhere. At eulogies you hear litanies of the material and passing allusions to compassion. Religion??? Gotta be careful...

What were you meant to be?... rings in my ears... did you achieve it? Did you figure out what life is all about and make sure you fulfilled your promise?

Somehow I feel that journeys end too soon. Life just can't be about the last years of golf... or finding a good church, and watching your pennies. Who were you meant to be? Or who could you have been???

Did you stand up for what is right? Did you define good and fight evil?

I have an intriguing résumé: Yale, Navy SEALs (UDT), great daughters, great travels, finishing with my wife's incredible business story. Who would have believed???

Yet all this would be meaningless if someone did not mention Jesus and my extraordinary involvement with

Him. Only the few know I was His rogue apostle chosen to lead others out of the walls that kept them from being splendid spiritual butterflies. That is the story worth telling. Joys to share with others that transcends all other relationships. Boy, was I blessed to have the perseverance to not quit on God. If I were alive during my eulogy I would shout out loud, "Don't quit on Jesus!"...

What you can't yet see is just around the corner if you keep moving forward.

Godspeed & love,

Dad

"Eyes"

The "I's" have it… or the "Aye's" have it. Or the "Eye's" have it.

Well, then??? Who has it? Who has the Truth??? I want to see it with my own eyes. Then I will believe it. Then I will know what the Truth is. But sometimes… yes… sometimes you don't get to see it with your own eyes.

The first assertion "The 'I's' have it" is really interesting. People tell us they believe or they saw it and we are to believe them. This is based on their "I." Their person. Their ego???

How many times do we rely on the "I" of another person to validate something? The witness of someone else to be the definer of Truth. We then are relying on another "I" to be honest. Interesting… But what about only trusting what you see with your own "eyes"???

The nautical nature of "Aye, Aye, Sir" brings up another notion in this sea of life and Truth we are exploring. "Aye,

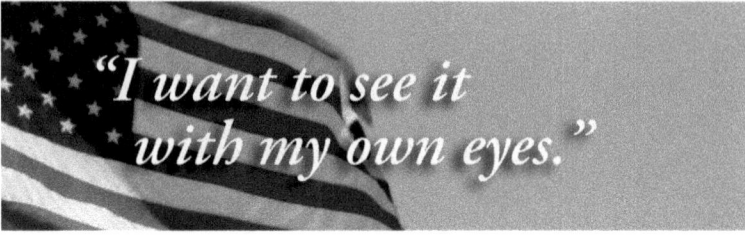

> "I want to see it
> with my own eyes."

Aye" means "Yes, I will do as directed." There is a truth in that.

In the US Senate you vote "Aye" or "Nay," yes or no. Something passes when the "Aye's have it." Something becomes law.

Right now we have this absurd impasse with debt and direction. A lot of "I's" have to say "Aye" for clarity to emerge and we can see with our own "eyes" what our future looks like. But we have to first agree upon values for an "Aye" to be relevant to Truth and our survival.

We are stripping our walls of our first beliefs. We don't know where to look anymore to find unison. Today pot is praised and cigarettes are banished. The family is legal fodder. Entitlement abuse is destroying initiative.

The "Aye's" have proclaimed the "I's" the victor. I am seeing it with my own eyes.

"Lincoln"

I just saw "Lincoln".

I just saw our Lincoln for the first time not in marble.

I just saw our nation born in values by a man assassinated.

This brooding film mostly about conversation and perseverance is disturbing and unfamiliar in its darkness and lack of action. Yet, it is a newborn masterpiece that brings us into a man of deep character who refused to be stuck in the mud of racism. You leave the theatre thanking God that Lincoln lived just long enough to get the vote passed. What would our nation be for the Negro had he caved in to the enormous political storm at the ending of the Civil War?

Equality at last for the slave. Absolutely unheard of. Yet here we are still with its vestiges and sensitivities. White and black alike are carving out colorless relationships. I have seen much of the good, but know that lingering pains lie beneath surfaces.

Subtle vestiges of racial snobbery and stereotyping continue to exist. The entitlement cancer hurts one more than the other. The drug decimation of the parent and family has insured racial discord as the fatherless child is reared in less than acceptable conditions.

Why are we so naive to think we can legislate the lack of love away? Who chucked proven values out the window?

Who liberated the liberal from his liberal forefather's commitment to rights? Genius move I must say. Conservatives are liberals. They too want what is good for all. It's as if a guilty conscience governs prudence rather than commitment to beliefs. We are lost again.

"Four score and seven years ago our fathers brought forth on this continent a new nation conceived in liberty and dedicated to the proposition that all men are created equal." The Gettysburg Address as prefaced by Abraham Lincoln. Equality and clarity period.

What more do we need in Washington?

Let's send our Navy SEALs there to rescue us from ourselves.

"Made in America"

I was made in America.

I was born in New York. I was not born in Africa. I was not born in China. I was not born in Iran. I was not born in Mexico. How come I was not born in Siberia? I don't know. But I'd like to meet the Guy who made the decision and shake His hand.

Why does everyone want to come here? Can't they just leave us alone and solve their own problems? We did ours… Kill off as many of your own as you want. Just leave us alone. We will even provide a little foreign aid for you if you do. We don't have anything you can't have. Liberty, justice, and freedom for all. Just do it. Equality? Human rights? Just words that make so much common sense that everyone understands. Capiche??? So get on with it. Google all you need to structure your country like ours… cast some votes… throw out the bad guys… show women some respect… and be kind to animals… and… you may get even more foreign aid.

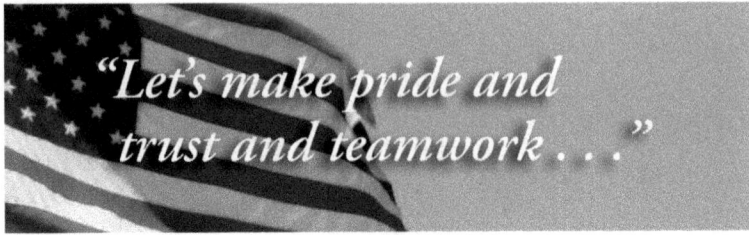

Ok America, what the heck is wrong with you? Why are you setting such a bad example to the rest of the world? Great job in managing family without fathers. Great job in legalizing nonsense and pot, metaphorically speaking. Great job in legalizing the legalizing of everything so fine print is your new god. Great job in idol worship at the expense of value worship.

Yet everyone still wants to be Born in the USA... (Thanks, Bruce). Go figure. Now we used to give birth to all kinds of product in the USA. But somewhere greed took over and managements in both business and labor started to get paid much more than they should. The rest is history. But everyone wants to become an American citizen. (I hope it is not for the entitlements...)

You know we put a man on the moon. I'll just bet we could build factories in our homeland and put man back to work. I'll just bet CEO's could make it happen if their bonuses were at stake. And, by the way, they aren't the bad guys, they are the good guys... if they would reconnect with their values. Their leadership is essential. But they must work alongside the worker, shoulder to shoulder, to build mutual respect. Ask a veteran how it works. Ask a Navy SEAL how it works.

Made in America. Heck, let's make everything in America. Let's make pride and trust and teamwork more than chalk on a Harvard blackboard.

"Am I in Trouble Dear"

I felt something as soon as she came in the room. Am I in trouble dear? I know I had done nothing. What could it be? I waited. Of course I am the only male to ever have said that.

Before they put their white dresses on we were never in trouble. And before they put their white dresses on we had never heard the word "shopping"??? Men don't discuss these things as they are the taboos of reality. A paradigm shift from being the hunter, provider, and protector that we so enjoyed as we guided our fiancée through the treacherous social caverns of pre-nuptial single life. Holding hands, warning one another of impending social bumps in the road. Eyes a-twinkle with innocence and passion. Moments of eternal bliss. The kiss.

"Honey," she says… "I have to go to my wedding dress fitting… see you later." Later was a good while. It seems that she also had her girlfriends to dine with. Years since, I sit in the parking lot of TJ Maxx, reading my iPad, checking my watch as she did say "I'll be right out dear" over an hour ago.

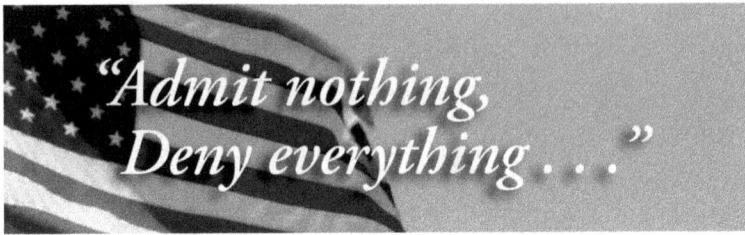

Now there are kids and all kinds of demands on time on top of commuting and work. But I am the hunter, provider and protector, skilled in the yard and waxing cars and errands. No problem. I catch the harried look as she shuts the door. Immediately I search my memory for incongruous circumstances that may give me a clue as to what will be immediately happening. Inside I sense I may have done something wrong. So I take the initiative and ask "How is your mother dear?"

To which she responds... "Why are you asking about her?" in a confrontational tone. Oops. What to do? Agonizing hesitation. Counter thrust. Change subject.

"Just wondering... Hey did the kids like the soccer game?

"Am I in trouble dear?"

Someone said this works: "Admit nothing, Deny everything. Make counter accusations." It was the motto of some intelligence agency...

"First Step"

Why does everything have to have a first step? Even a baby's first step is so hard. Remember??? Of course not. But from looking at children taking their first steps we can remember the lack of balance and confidence. They did not know where that first step would take them. Amazing in hindsight.

Akin to getting on a bike for the first time. Or like jumping in a pool for the first time. I had no clue it would propel me to diving down in the night and into a submarine.

Then there are the first steps one takes into where one is warned not to go. There is the first step into passion, be it a hobby, sport, or the other kind. Those are easy steps propelled by urge and desire.

We act as if we are in control of the future and can never take a first step that is wrong, don't we??? Maybe the first step is arrogance? Maybe the first step is denial of caution? And maybe the first step is plain old ignorance.

" . . . your first step has to be the right one . . ."

We have icons of success to follow, emulate, and ponder. They flash on screens, large and small, all day long. There are celebrities in every form of activity. I want to be like... Children dream of becoming like... We are told you can be what you want to be... You can have dreams that come true. It is just that your first step has to be the right one... and then the next... and the next. All of us can look back on the choices made, for each is a step in a direction. You want to be an Air Force Pilot? There are steps and people to explain them. You want to be a professional singer? There are steps... You want to be a doctor? A lawyer??? A pastor???

More importantly, do you want to make a difference? Do you want to be known for doing good or for doing nothing? Or bad? Important choices. The choice is the important first step. How do you make it??? Well... You Just Do It!

One can do first step research by asking the right person what his first step was and if it was hard to make. You will get amazing stories. No two the same. And yours will be like none other.

Life is made up of single steps… one hour and one day at a time. This is how it works. Quitting along the way yields nothing and invalidates all that preceded. The first step must have some positive rationale. There must be some good associated. There must be some chosen value to make it worthwhile. To have value it has to intend good. One has to decide that good is good and what good is. For good has power, and good has meaning. Your first step has to be about good.

Look around you and see what you hold to be good. Then you can form a value system upon which to propel your first step. It will also make where you are going clearer.

Oh, and find some good shoes as there are a lot of obstacles to doing good. People will step on your feet and your first steps.

Hurry up. I am waiting for you.

"Rights Abuse"

Let's form a new special interest group, the SPCR. The Society for the Prevention of Cruelty to Rights. I am so sick and tired of rights being abused, watered down, and used as issues against the majority. Whew... this is really dangerous terrain...???

Let's amend the Right to have Rights. Let's define that the majority oppresses all minority interests and feelings. Let us raise the smallest group of like-minded to decide the rights of all who feel differently. There is no more room for good unless it is the minority. Where nothing has value unless it has no value. Bet I got you with this... LOL.

We can make anything legal that we want... unless of course, it is opposed by a sincere self-interest group.

Sound like chaos??? Well, step back... and let's be honest... absurdity is approaching.

If your values are not mine, then yours are wrong.

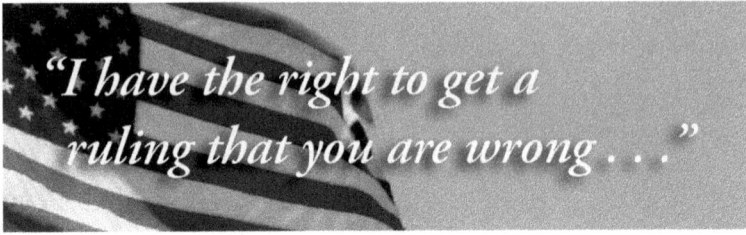

I am so thankful we have a Supreme Court to help us decide if our rights are right. But all it takes is one vote to the contrary and my rights are wrong. Is that right? For one person to decide the fate of another??? Much less a majority???

Of course you have the right to say that I am wrong, but I have the right to get a ruling that you are wrong. And the SPCR is behind me! Unless they think I am being cruel to your rights… LOL.

If my wife wants to shop at midnight on Sundays who has the right to deny her shopping rights? Aren't her feelings and needs important too??? What is a right? Can some court define better??? I have a right to fight for her rights.

We need Lincoln back. We have become slaves to rights.

"Don't Tell Anyone"

I remember this old, now really old TV show called The Millionaire. Stories about a wealthy man who came across people in trouble and he took care of their problem or debt without them knowing… and moved on. I was so impressed with this. This fictional guy was just cool. That is the way to do it. Unseen. Asking not for thanks. Chivalry? Heroic? Dignified? Classy? I think we would say yes to all…

In combat as in life… or in the combat of life individuals do heroic things. Even to giving up their lives for others. Most all ask not for recognition. The profound force of humility usually makes them lower their heads as if shy and say it was just the right and only thing to do. Moving…

When you are around this type of person you feel good. Because you feel that you are close to right. You are close to values… or good… or what life ennobled can be…

In our celebrity "me" driven culture we want recognition for everything we do. Texting affirmation to one another as if character and confidence are just a keystroke away.

"It's between me and my Maker . . ."

We love award ceremonies where everyone pats one's self on the back. Hey, the Pulitzer Prize just went to the European Union for disunity or some achievement hard to explain. Hands are shaken. Cocktails consumed. Limos depart. I don't know why we have to dress up for charity events and go to fancy parties to celebrate our generosity. What happened to the manly old way of writing a check in private? Handing it to the recipient and saying "Don't tell anyone." Put the money to best use immediately. "Don't tell anyone." It's between me and my Maker…

Then there is the syndrome of others knowing what one has given. Are you on the Diamond or Platinum or Gold or Silver List of Patrons??? If you are on the Diamond are you making the Silver Patrons uncomfortable or jealous??? On the dance floor are there sections for each? Do only the Diamonds get to waltz???

My boat is bigger than yours.

Don't tell anyone.

"Fiscal Cliff"

To Hire or Not To Hire, that is the question. Small businesses have been dealt a strange deck of cards.

The top of the deck says USA Government with a lovely flag motif. When you get to the face and number of the card there is neither order nor sequential design. Hearts are health insurance, Clubs are expenses, Spades are taxes, and Diamonds are promises. But there are no numbers on them. So who can play?

Your deal. Five card stud. Simple. Better have a parachute.

"Stand Up! Hook Up!

Equipment Check!

Sound Off!

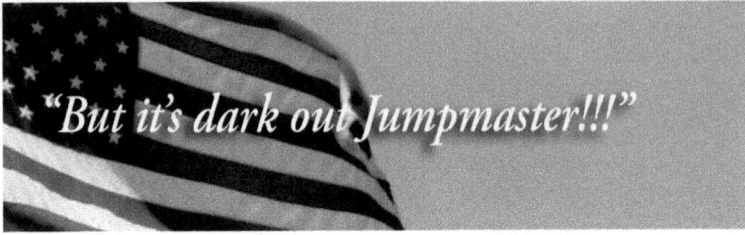

Stand In The Door!"

"But it's dark out Jumpmaster!!!

I can't see the ground."

"The Résumé"

I really didn't believe it. I had heard stories, but I really couldn't conceive of what we have allowed to come to pass. An attractive e-mail is received inquiring about work with a résumé attached. I responded to call and have an interview with us. She came in only to say she wasn't interested. She just needed us as an entry to her "log" to maintain unemployment qualification. This is now common practice. Entitlement is a beautiful thing for the truly deserving. Yet, there are so many entitlement opportunities that are being played by a growing percent of the population... We now need a new bureaucracy for entitlement abuse. How can someone behind a government desk discern who is playing them? Paperwork begets paperwork and becomes the enemy of truth. Multiple sign-offs on documents neuters accountability and responsibility and shields fraud from discovery.

Of course, there would then have to be an investigation process, potentially leading to legal involvement, with both sides' attorneys being compensated by the government.

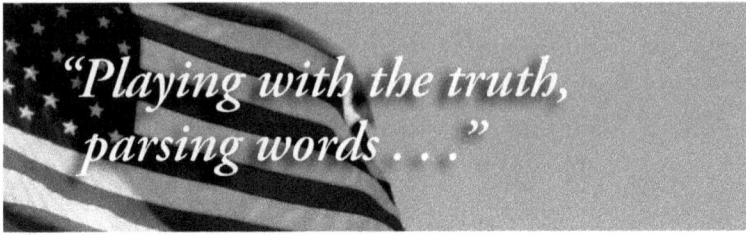

Who will accuse? Who will follow through? How many hearings? Will the police have to police the absurd?

We do not have the infrastructure to investigate ourselves. We have abrogated our rights to an onerous system. Our values used to be the checkpoint. Many more had values and there still existed an ancient psycho-mechanism called conscience. It worked until we killed it by labeling it as harmful, by labeling it as guilt.

We have great labor unions which originally were value driven organizations dedicated to fairness. But they grew their fat paychecks and infrastructure and became managers of self-interest rather than humble servants of the worker.

The scandals of the finance industry are so shameful that they defy comment. Shame on all who looked the other way. It was a three card Monte Wall Street hustle. But what has made us a country now becoming a leader in work avoidance? With e-mail and texting it is sure easier to create a false paper and communication trail of sham effort. Playing with the truth, parsing words and intent, manufacturing qualifications, embellishing experience... How has this become acceptable??

"Fun"

I just got back from the Village School where a bunch of kids were sorting donated toys. What a buzz of joyous activity as Christmas was being bagged for families who had little for their own Christmas tree, metaphorically speaking. Must have been 60 kids, teenagers, who knew they were doing it for the less fortunate and they were having fun. It feels good to do good. It feels good to form values.

It feels good to have values. This is a good school. Good seeds are planted. Fun.

Why have we made life so non-fun except for beer and sports? (Metaphorically speaking.) Why is it that when we help others we feel truly good? Why is it that when we help ourselves we feel only transparently good? When we help ourselves to another portion of self we get physically and mentally fat... and create less appetite to do unselfish good. Not as much fun.

We used to look in the mirror and see ourselves. Now we just look at our whatever and get back to texting or whatever.

If good seeds are planted young enough, then a kid has a chance at surviving life and its self-centered urges. So, of course, with all our self-appointed wisdom we are legislating the content of schoolbooks and laying barren the soil for good seeds.

Now... a good seed has to be like the mustard seed and somehow survive on rocky ground.

Why have the parents abrogated their values to a suspect judiciary? We are legislating mediocrity and inadvertently providing a lack of diversity of values and opinion. This is intellectual racism when you make Christian values unwelcome and infer that they are evil. Bigoted racism.

Why is non-faith better than faith? Who says?

I have been blessed with a journey that has not seen the real poverty or felt the real pain of the majority. Please don't judge me by the immaterial, much less the material. I was born in Bronxville, NY in 1940. Grew up in Louisville and St Louis. Graduated from Yale and went into the Navy. I had the great honor of fulfilling my dream to become a Frogman. I graduated from BUDS Class 31E, Basic Underwater Demolition/Seal School. I was an officer in Underwater Demolition Team 21 which became Seal Team 4 in 1984. I had the honor of recovering several spacecraft, including Gemini 6/7 & AS-201, the very first Apollo Spacecraft to go into space. Wow, did I luck out. Then I spent 40 years in women's retail, in various department stores. Even a year at the World Wrestling Federation... go figure?

I have two great daughters and two grandchildren who have just discovered the water and facemasks. My wife has created probably the #1 women's accessory store in the country as evidenced by how much she is copied. Therein I work and report to her... No comment. LOL.

As you can tell by reading between the lines there is a spiritual side to my journey. Kind of covert as I just want to make a difference unseen.

God Bless You All… Happy Trails.

ACKNOWLEDGEMENTS

Families matter more than ever.

They are being torn apart by politics.

Our grandchildren and great-great grandchildren are looking to us to show them the path to Truth....

Please read every chapter privately, please....

My short list of contributors:

My daughters, Candice and Courtney, who have much more to learn about their dad. There is my brilliant wife Christina who continued to inadvertently mold me. And there are my friends from the past whose life journeys I do not fully know, and who do not know me now. For in life we are who we become, not who we were.

Then there are the men of my "No Walls" Bible Studies, and Max Lucado who freed us to think with assurance and humility, leading me to new friendships of the highest quality. Durrenberger, Lord, Wood among many others.

There are the veterans I served with and those I didn't: Ames, Riojas, Stevens, Cleary, Cofield, Diviney, Bisset,

Shapira, Fry, Ross, Hawes, Hawkins, Heaphy, Hernandez, Bruton, Olson, Vecchione, Phillips, Waddel, Blais, Sutherland, and my brothers in UDT/R BUD/S 31E and countless others.... Where bonding and trust was defined.

Lastly, there is Sandra Simmons-Dawson, President of Customer Finder Marketing, who helped edit and format the books, website, and marketing.

Chris Bent

Naples
September 2013
www.chrisbent.com

IN THE WORDS OF OTHERS

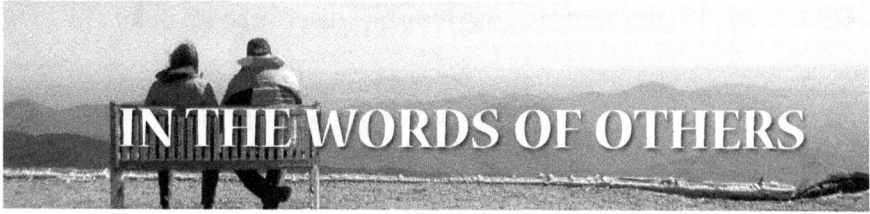

"This is a book by a man of many directions and passions. Straightforward yet thought provoking. Loyal to his convictions and country. And brave. Sharing. Warrior. Humanitarian."

Jeff Lytle, Editorial Page Editor, Naples Daily News

"As a friend, Chris has helped me understand the inherent conflicts embedded in the language of 'political correctness' and how it attempts, and frequently succeeds, in disguising and defeating the 'truth.' Chris is engaged in a rhetorical battle — we need his insight."

William Lord, a 32-year-veteran Executive Producer
and Vice-President of ABC News, and
Professor of Journalism at Boston University

"Chris writes like he lives. As a man of distinction, he is a voice for the poor, a champion of the truth and a friend of strong character and conviction. His word and his service are a blessing to all who encounter him."

Vann R. Ellison, President/CEO, St. Matthew's House, Inc.

"My nickname for Chris is "Dream-Catcher"- because that's who he is to me. He is my mentor in how to give on His behalf. Freely and generously, Chris offers both words, "God bless you!", and gifts. And all the while he is making a compelling and powerful statement. Chris Bent has discovered a beautiful way to live!"

Rev. Dr. Ruth Merriam, The Church on the Cape (U.M.C.),
Cape Porpoise, Maine — Chris's 'other' pastor!

"Chris Bent is a very unusual person – Navy SEAL, Yale graduate, successful business owner, and radical Christian who is comfortable talking with anyone at any level in society. He doesn't just talk about faith or caring about the poor, Chris actually lives his faith and he works with the poor. His smile is genuine and reflects his deep joy in life, America, hard work, people and (most definitely) God. I have enjoyed reading his writings; they are different, often hard hitting and sometimes maybe even a little wild. Each one gives a fresh perspective on contemporary lives, reflecting Chris' intelligence and faith. Chris enjoys moving mountains."

Rev. Dr. Ted Sauter, Senior Pastor,
North Naples United Methodist Church

www.ingramcontent.com/pod-product-compliance
Lightning Source LLC
Chambersburg PA
CBHW050110280326
41933CB00010B/1047